從羽神到熔爐

The Mystreious Hawai'i

From the Feathered Gods the Melting Pot

Preface
館長序

從羽神到熔爐

檀島傳奇
The Mystreious Hawai'i
From the Feathered Gods the Melting Pot

精采動人Aloha：記檀島傳奇特展

在遙遠的太平洋上有幾座大小不一的島嶼，它們的緯度跟台灣差不多，但它孤懸在浩瀚的海洋之間，距離最近的大陸有2500哩，是許多人夢中理想的樂園。夏威夷群島主要由夏威夷島（Hawai'i island）、歐胡（O'ahu）、茂宜（Maui）、考艾（Kaua'i）等島嶼所組成。在椰林下展現迷人舞姿、海灘衝浪、火山探險、雨林尋幽，大概是每一個曾經到過夏威夷的人最直接的印象。

大約在西元500年到700年左右，最早的夏威夷人就已經到達，這一批也許是移動速度最快的南島語族。接著，在1000年左右，大溪地人（Tahitians）到島上定居。1778年，庫克（James Cook）船長到達歐胡等島嶼，夏威夷被西方「發現」了，從此也開始它新的命運。在卡美哈美哈（Kamehameha）王朝五世代的管理下，夏威夷曾有過長期的和平歲月。19世紀中葉，亞洲和中南美洲各國開始移民夏威夷，造成民族血統與文化的融合，現在大約有三分之一的夏威夷人說自己是混合民族（Mixed Ethnicity）。1959年，夏威夷成為美國第50州。

在檀香山市的比夏博物館（Bishop Museum）是夏威夷最大的博物館，收藏上百萬件夏威夷和太平洋地區的各類文物標本。本館為了讓國內關心多元族群文化之美，卻無緣到夏威夷參觀的朋友能親身體會夏威夷的人文之美，便在2005年開始規劃與比夏博物館合作的相關事宜；策展及協調工作由張至善、喬宗忞擔任；展示的內容經由比夏博物館副館長 Betty Kam 女士和本館的喬宗忞、張至善商議，以夏威夷的歷史為主題進行展示設計，涵蓋非常豐富的物質、精神與社群等各層面文化的內涵，並由張至善、袁素梅規劃教育活動，以擴張展示的效果；而文物標本需要跨海來去，點交、運輸與維護工作就由葉前錦、徐雨村、夏麗芳、林建成、劉世龍、張至善處理；工務機電組楊宗瑋、秘書室魯玉玲協助發包事宜；標本文物的上、下架由方鈞瑋、葉前錦及研究典藏組同仁負責；公共服務組第一線的導覽人員也在經由學習的過程之後，擔負解說任務；所以為了讓這項展覽順利呈現，本館全體同仁都付出相當多的心力，也為爾後辦理國際合作增添寶貴的經驗。感謝所有促成這次特展的人士和本館同仁。特展已經結束，特輯即將付梓，謹綴數言以誌其事。

浦忠成

巴蘇亞・博伊哲努

pasuya・poiconu

Preface
比夏博物館序

從羽神到熔爐

檀島傳奇
The Mystreious Hawai'i
From the Feathered Gods the Melting Pot

Aloha kākou!

It is indeed a pleasure to share a part of our Hawaiian ancestry and treasures with family across the Pacific, and Bishop Museum is most honored to have worked with the National Museum of Prehistory in Taiwan in this endeavor.

The exhibition, titled ***The Mysterious Hawaiʻi, from the Feathered Gods to the Melting Pot,*** provides a look at who the Hawaiians were and who they have come to be. Their identity is seen in the works of their hands, the passion of their skills, their wisdom expressed in art. Their story starts in legendary times and is tracked to modern practices in the Hawaiʻi of today. Artifacts for this exhibition were carefully selected to entice the visitor to ask the larger question, "How are Hawaiians and other Pacific peoples related to the people of Taiwan and China?" It is this mystery that is now being aggressively pursued as archaeologists collect data and form postulation on that ancient relationship.

Bishop Museum is especially grateful and acknowledges those dedicated staff at Taiwan's National Museum of Prehistory who over the expanse of thousands of miles, worked "hand-in-hand," and, regardless of the difference in language, depended on minds that worked in rhythm with those at Bishop Museum to create this exhibition. A special thank you is sent to the Museum's Director and to all his dedicated staff, Trai, Rai-Ming (崔瑞明), Chiao, Tsung-Min (喬宗忞), Hsu, Yu-Tsuen (徐雨村), Yeh, Chian-Jin, (葉前錦), Shia, Li-Fang (夏麗芳), Chang, Chi-Shan (張至善), Lin, Puja (林妙香), Fang, Chun-Wei (方鈞瑋), Liu, Shih-Lung (劉世龍), which supported the development of the exhibition and for the gracious hospitality they provided. Hawai i (and its treasured artifacts) felt right at home in the midst of Taitung's exquisite and beautiful museum!

The experience of developing and completing this project is in itself a lesson in the study of cultures that appear separated by miles, yet connected by the same interests, same curiosity, and a shared impulse to seek what is common among different peoples.

Betty Lou Kam

Vice President, Cultural Resources

目錄

從羽神到熔爐

檀島傳奇
The Mystreious Hawai'i
From the Feathered Gods the Melting Pot

創世紀・神話
Creation・Mythology

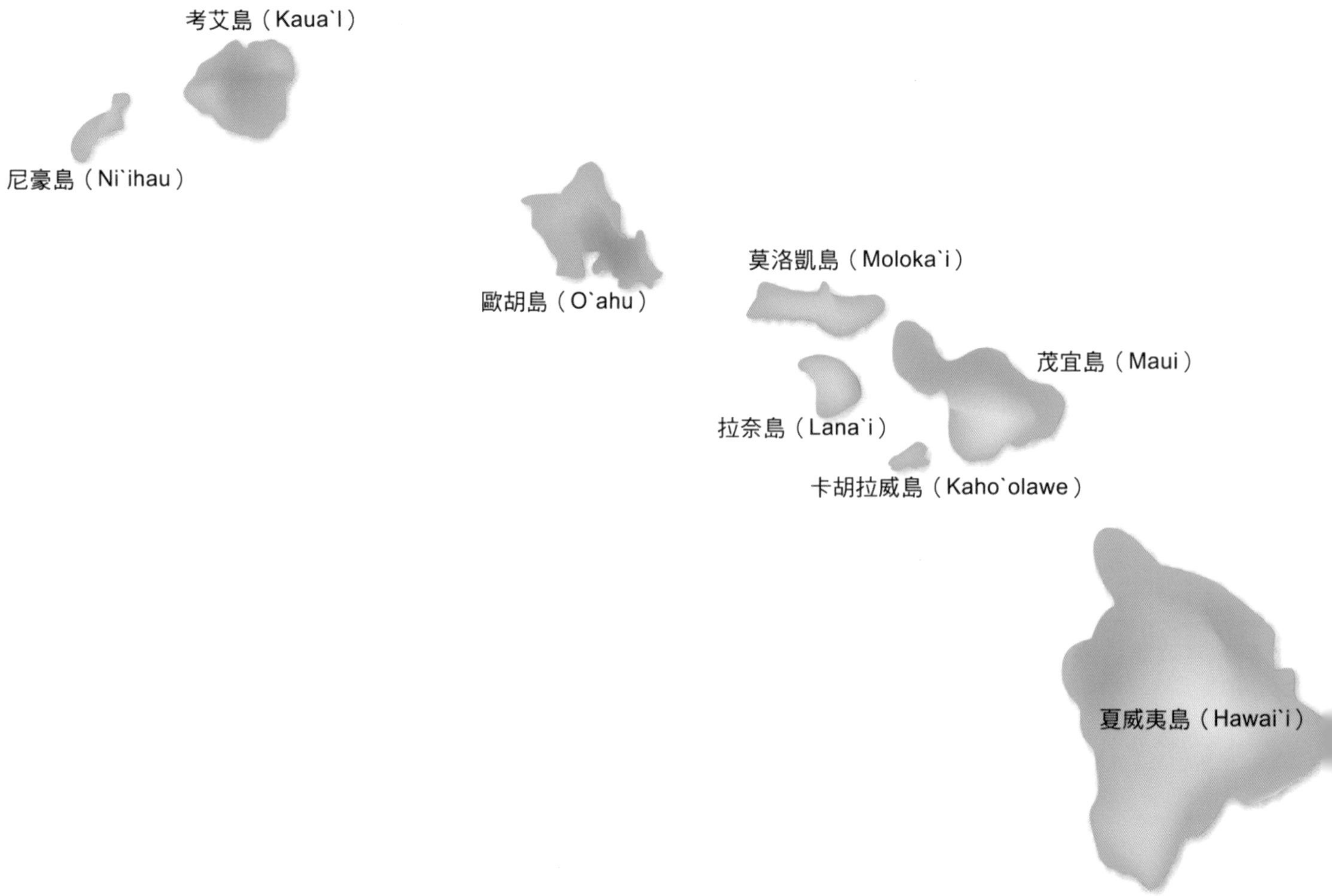

考艾島（Kaua`l）

尼豪島（Ni`ihau）

歐胡島（O`ahu）

莫洛凱島（Moloka`i）

茂宜島（Maui）

拉奈島（Lana`i）

卡胡拉威島（Kaho`olawe）

夏威夷島（Hawai`i）

夏威夷群島的誕生神話

夏威夷群島與島上的所有人都是從精靈世界誕生。父母是大地「帕帕」（Papa）與天空(或宇宙)「哇凱亞」（Wakea），第一個誕生的孩子是夏威夷島，接著是茂宜島（Maui）、卡侯歐拉威島（Kaho'olawe）。之後，帕帕返回大溪地，哇凱亞娶了其他妻子。卡烏拉（Ka'ula）為他生下拉奈島（Lana'i），希娜（Hina）為他生了第五個孩子莫洛凱島（Moloka'i）。

聽到哇凱亞有了新妻子的消息後，帕帕很快便從大溪地回來。由於嫉妒，她開始與路阿（Lua）來往，並生下歐胡島（O'ahu）。最後，哇凱亞與帕帕復合，考艾島（Kaua'i）、尼豪島（Ni'ihau）、卡烏拉島（Ka'ula）、尼侯阿島（Nihoa）於是誕生，至此，夏威夷群島的主要島嶼鍊就完成了。

The mythological birth of the Hawaiian Islands

The islands of Hawai`i and all their people were born of the spirit world. The parents were Papa, the earth, and Wakea, sky or space. Their first born child was the island of Hawai`i, and the next was Maui, then Kaho`olawe. Papa returned to Tahiti and Wakea took other wives. Ka'ula bore him the island of Lana`i, and with Hina, he created a fifth child, the island of Moloka`i.

Hearing of Wakea's new wives, Papa quickly returned from Tahiti. In a fit of jealousy, she took up with Lua and gave birth to the island of O`ahu. The couple, Wakea and Papa, was finally reunited and the islands of Kaua`i, Ni`ihau, Ka'ula and Nihoa resulted, thus completing the chain of major Hawaiian Islands.

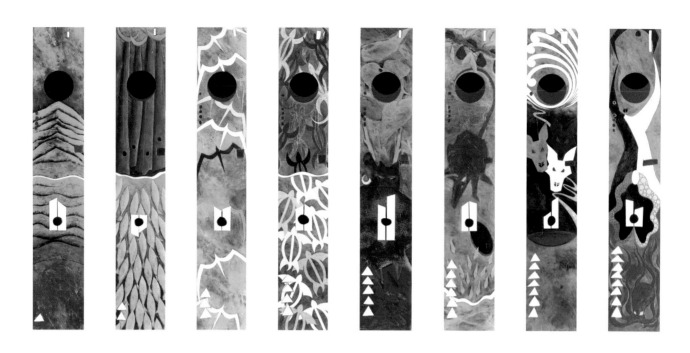

庫木里玻

庫木里玻的字面意義是：生命的源頭或起源，它表現最早的夏威夷人對起源的了解，以及這個群島上的生命發展。這些頌詩的目的是讓夏威夷的「阿里伊」（a li`i，酋長）在系譜關係上連結到大自然，也連結到他們和其他玻里尼西亞人共有的神祇。它基本上是一個家族頌詩，但也證實了夏威夷人的哲理，並讓我們了解他們當時所居住的世界。

今日，庫木里玻讓夏威夷人連結到他們的系譜關係：從一隻珊瑚蟲開始延伸，帶出水底深處的世界，到達陸地，最後是人類與酋長階級的發展。這些引發討論的想法與概念，鼓舞了研究夏威夷文化的人。

卡爾・坡（Carl F. K. Pao）是一位夏威夷當代藝術家，他從幾個庫木里玻英文翻譯版，創造出視覺化的詮釋。但最主要的依據還是大衛・卡拉卡瓦國王（King David Kalākaua）譯於1880年代的版本，以及瑪莎・貝克衛詩（Martha Beckwith）在1951年的最新翻譯版。

他創作了庫木里玻的藝術作品，希望它能：『發揮作用，成為一個對文化、對祖先、同輩，以及後輩負起責任的作品。』卡爾・坡許諾要創造生動、獨特，而且是夏威夷文化、土地和人民所特有的藝術作品。

The Kumulipo

The *Kumulipo* (literally, the origin or source of life) expressed the very earliest Hawaiian understanding of the origins and development of life in the Islands. The purpose of the chant is to genealogically link Hawaiian *ali'i* (chiefs) to nature and to the gods shared with other Polynesians. It is basically a family chant, but one that provides evidence of Hawaiian philosophy and understanding of the world in which they lived.

Today, the *Kumulipo* connects Hawaiians to their lineage, a succession that extends from a coral polyp, leads out of the watery depths to land, and ends with the development of man and the *ali'i* class. It inspires students of Hawaiian culture with provocative thought and concepts.

Carl F. K. Pao, a contemporary Hawaiian artist, created his visual interpretation of the *Kumulipo* based on various translations, but based largely on the work of King David Kalākaua in the 1880s, and the more recent translation by Martha Beckwith (1951). Pao's intention for *Kumulipo*, his work of art, is for it to "function as a piece responsible to our culture, to my ancestors, to my peers, and those that will follow." Pao is committed to creating works of art that are dynamic and unique, yet specific to the Hawaiian culture, land, and people.

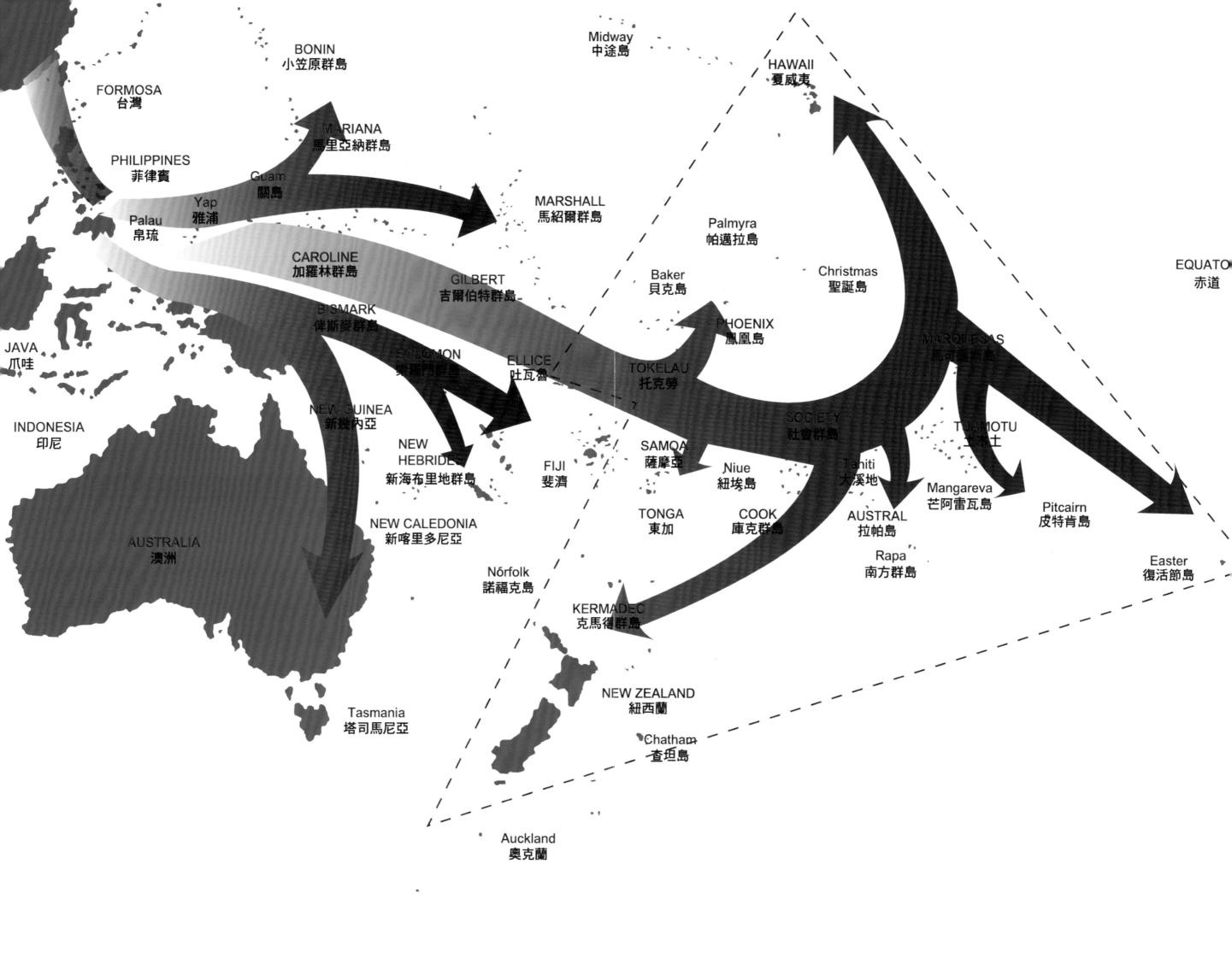

BONIN
小笠原群島

Midway
中途島

HAWAII
夏威夷

FORMOSA
台灣

MARIANA
馬里亞納群島

PHILIPPINES
菲律賓

Guam
關島

Yap
雅浦

Palau
帛琉

MARSHALL
馬紹爾群島

Palmyra
帕邁拉島

EQUATO
赤道

CAROLINE
加羅林群島

GILBERT
吉爾伯特群島

Baker
貝克島

Christmas
聖誕島

BISMARK
俾斯麥群島

JAVA
爪哇

SOLOMON
索羅門群島

ELLICE
吐瓦魯

TOKELAU
托克勞

PHOENIX
鳳凰島

MARQUESAS
馬可薩斯島

INDONESIA
印尼

NEW GUINEA
新幾內亞

NEW
HEBRIDES
新海布里地群島

FIJI
斐濟

SAMOA
薩摩亞

Niue
紐埃島

SOCIETY
社會群島

TUAMOTU
土木土

NEW CALEDONIA
新喀里多尼亞

Tahiti
大溪地

Mangareva
芒阿雷瓦島

Pitcairn
皮特肯島

AUSTRALIA
澳洲

Norfolk
諾福克島

TONGA
東加

COOK
庫克群島

AUSTRAL
拉帕島

Rapa
南方群島

Easter
復活節島

KERMADEC
克馬得群島

Tasmania
塔司馬尼亞

NEW ZEALAND
紐西蘭

Chatham
查垣島

Auckland
奧克蘭

在太平洋的遷徙

Migration through the Pacific

探索太平洋人群的起源

不同領域的研究人員已經論證出：中國的東南地區是南島語族（玻里尼西亞人、美拉尼西亞人、密克羅尼西亞和東南亞諸島的原住民）最初的家園。考古上的證據指出，居住在中國此一區域的人民具有非凡的航海能力與技術，他們的史前航海遊歷標示了：南島語族及其後代子孫遷移至太平洋各地的開端。

這些精通航海的旅人，從亞洲大陸往東行，然後在太平洋地區定居下來，最後的落腳處是美拉尼西亞和密克羅尼西亞，並延伸到玻里尼西亞。這些冒險的水手們在長距離海洋航程中考驗其技能，他們學習解讀海鳥的飛翔途徑、風向、海流和星象，進而標下他們的路線。許多航海者都是為了找尋一個新家園、一種和平安詳的生活方式，以及可靠的食物來源。

太平洋各地人們的關係，可從他們的語言和物質文化的相似性與差異性看出。有些考古學家研究那些線索，提出這些人在太平洋各地遷徙的模式，以及遷移的大略順序。

Exploring the origins of the peoples of the Pacific

Researchers in various fields have demonstrated that Southeast China is the original homeland of the Austronesians (Polynesians, Melanesians , Micronesians and indigenous people of Southeast Asian Archipelagos). Archaeological evidence indicates the people of this area in China had remarkable seafaring skills and technology . Their prehistoric voyaging marks the start of the movement made by Austronesians and their descendants throughout the Pacific.

The Pacific was settled by skilled wayfarers who moved eastward from the Asian continent, eventually populating areas in Melanesia, Micronesia and reaching toward Polynesia . These adventurous sailors tested their skills in long distance ocean travel, learning to read the paths of birds, wind and sea currents, and the skies in order to mark their route. Many of those who sailed sought new homes, a peaceful lifestyle , and dependable sources of food.

The relationships among the people throughout the Pacific are suggested by the similarities and differences in language and material culture. Some archaeologists study such clues to propose patterns of migrations throughout the Pacific, and the approximate sequence of such movement.

大坌坑文化遺址

Site of Tapenkeng Culture

位於臺灣北部的大坌坑遺址是大坌坑文化最早被研究的地點。

南島語族的源頭

夏威夷與台灣的原住民同屬南島語系。研究者推測，夏威夷之南島語族祖先很可能源自包括台灣在內的中國東南沿岸一帶。台灣的考古學家已在台灣北部、南部、東部，以及澎湖群島發現了若干新石器時代早期遺址，出土裝飾繩紋的陶器、石錛，以及稻穀和小米等作物。這些遺留被稱作「大坌坑文化」，年代距今 5000- 6000年。著名的考古學家張光直先生認為這個文化可能是南島語族最早的祖先。而台灣的大坌坑文化可能是來自中國東南沿海。

The origins of the Austronesian-speaking Peoples

The indigenous peoples of Taiwan and Hawaiï speak the same Austronesian language. Researchers have postulated that the ancestors of the Hawaiian indigenes may have come from the areas of the southeast coast of China, including Taiwan, several thousand years ago. Taiwanese archaeologists have discovered quite a few early Neolithic sites in Taiwan and Penghu, from which pottery characterized by cord-impressed decorations, stone adzes as well as rice and millet grains are unearthed. These cultural remains have been named "Tapenkeng Culture" by the late Harvard Professor Kwang-chi Chang, who suggested that it represents most probably the earliest ancestors of the present day Austronesian-speaking peoples.

夏威夷男人挖掘馬鈴薯

Hawaiian man with ʻōʻō (digging stick) and sweet potato vines, Molokaʻi, Hawaiʻi.

太平洋各地的錛與斧

太平洋區的錛與斧反映出相似性和差異性。在大部分的太平洋地區，石斧與石錛都很普遍，但在不產玄武岩的地區，多半是密克羅尼西亞地區，工匠轉而使用強硬的硨磲蛤殼來製作錛斧的頭部。辨別材質、頭部形狀、綑綁的種類等特徵，研究者能夠了解錛斧的使用者來自何處。對於單一型式的廣泛研究，讓人得以對遷徙的模式以及與其他地區文化族群的關連產生新的想法。

Adzes from throughout the Pacific

Pacific adzes reflect similarities and differences. Stone adzes are prevalent over most of the Pacific, but in areas where good basalt is lacking, much of Micronesia, craftsman turned to strong Tridacna shell to fashion adze heads. Distinguishing characteristics, such as materials, the shape of the adze head, the kind of lashing used help researchers to understand the origins of people. A study of a broad range of a single type of object results in new ideas on the patterns of migration and associations with cultural groups from other areas.

美拉尼西亞　Melanesia 石斧，具有劈開的籐製把手。巴布新幾內亞的新不列顛島
Stone axe, hafted with split rattan, New Britain, Papua New Guinea

L64 × W18 × T7 cm

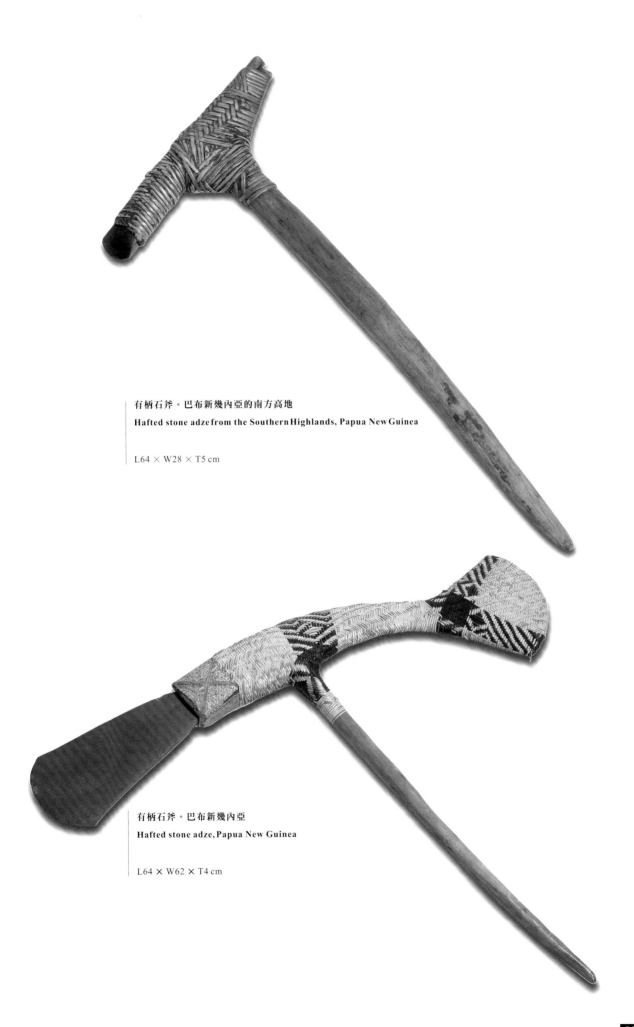

有柄石斧。巴布新幾內亞的南方高地
Hafted stone adze from the Southern Highlands, Papua New Guinea

L64 × W28 × T5 cm

有柄石斧。巴布新幾內亞
Hafted stone adze, Papua New Guinea

L64 × W62 × T4 cm

密克羅尼西亞　Micronesia

有柄硨磲蛤殼斧。吉里巴斯的吉爾伯特群島
Tridacna shell adze, hafted, Gilbert Islands, Kiribati

L41 × W22 × T4 cm

有柄硨磲蛤殼斧。密克羅尼西亞聯邦的土魯克島
Tridacna shell adze, hafted, Truk, Federated States of Micronesia

L55 × W33 × T8 cm

在大部分的太平洋地區，石斧與石錛都很普遍，但在
不產玄武岩的地區，多半是密克羅尼西亞，工匠轉而
使用強硬的硨磲蛤殼來製作錛斧的頭部。

Stone adzes are prevalent over most of the Pacific, but in areas where good
basalt is lacking, much of Micronesia, craftsman turned to strong Tridacna
shell to fashion adze heads.

玻里尼西亞　Polynesia

有柄硨磲蛤殼斧。所羅門群島的錫克亞納
Tridacna shell adze, hafted, Sikaiana, Solomon Islands (Polynesian Outlier)

L69 × W34 × T6 cm

有柄石錛。社會群島
Hafted adze from the Society Islands
L50 × W20 × T5.5 cm

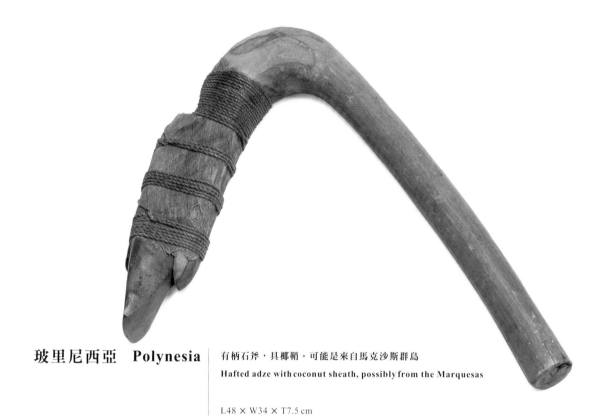

玻里尼西亞　Polynesia

有柄石斧，具椰鞘。可能是來自馬克沙斯群島
Hafted adze with coconut sheath, possibly from the Marquesas

L48 × W34 × T7.5 cm

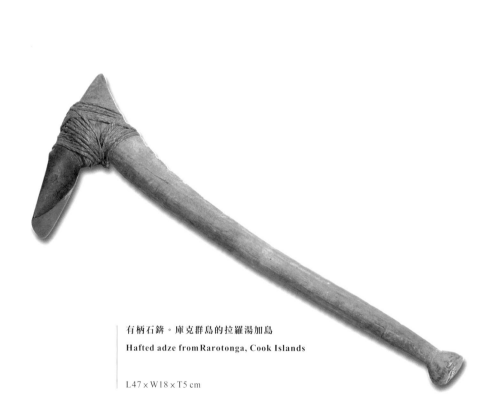

有柄石錛。庫克群島的拉羅湯加島
Hafted adze from Rarotonga, Cook Islands

L47 × W18 × T5 cm

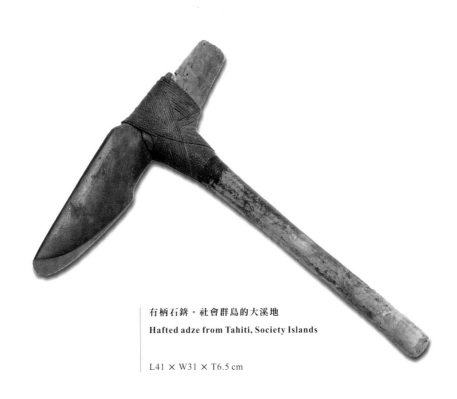

有柄石錛。社會群島的大溪地

Hafted adze from Tahiti, Society Islands

L41 × W31 × T6.5 cm

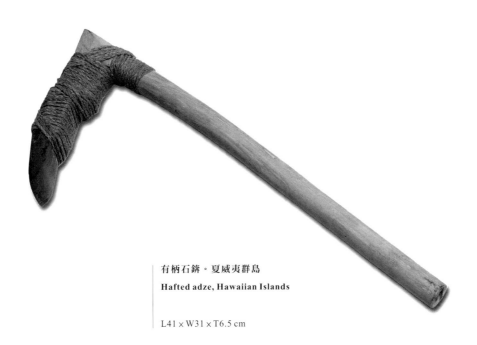

有柄石錛。夏威夷群島

Hafted adze, Hawaiian Islands

L41 × W31 × T6.5 cm

玻里尼西亞的魚鉤和誘餌

Polynesian fish hooks and lures

夏威夷的魚鉤是由骨頭、珍珠貝和龜殼製成。那些龜殼製的魚鉤又更加美麗，
許多此類龜殼製品皆為貿易目的所製作。

Hawaiian fishhooks were made from bone, pearl shell and turtle shell.

Those of turtle were especially beautiful, and many such shells were made for the purpose of trade.

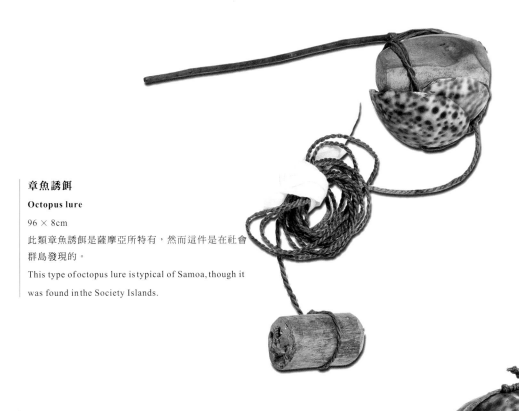

章魚誘餌
Octopus lure

96 × 8cm

此類章魚誘餌是薩摩亞所特有，然而這件是在社會
群島發現的。

This type of octopus lure is typical of Samoa, though it
was found in the Society Islands.

章魚誘餌 / 社會群島
Octopus lure, Society Islands

49.5 × 5.5cm

章魚會受到寶螺殼的吸引，當它進入殼內後，警覺的漁夫會快速地將誘餌和章魚從水裡拉出
夏威夷人使用的類似誘餌在最後被裝上鉤子。

The octopus is attracted by the cowry shell. The octopus settles on the shell,

and the watchful fisherman quickly pulls the lure and octopus out of the water.

Similar lures used in Hawai`i were eventually equipped with hooks.

章魚誘餌 / 社會群島
Octopus lure, Society Islands

37.5 × 7.5cm

這個誘餌並沒有使用完整的寶螺，而是將幾個片狀殼包覆起來，
綁在一支簡單的木棒上。

Rather than a full cowry shell, this lure holds plates of shell bundled
and attached to a simple wood stick.

魚誘餌 / 東加島

Fish lure, Tonga

8 × 1.5cm

拖曳誘餌來捕捉鰹魚，這在太平洋各地都是非常相似的。這件是由珍珠貝殼
和一個U型龜殼倒鉤製成。

Trolling lures to catch bonito were very similar throughout Polynesia.

This one is made of pearl shell with a u-shaped turtle shell barb.

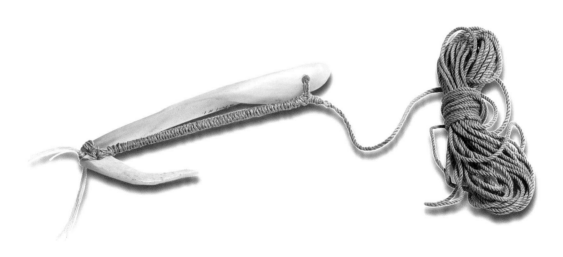

魚誘餌 / 夏威夷

Fish lure, Hawai`i

11.8 × 1.8cm

鰹魚誘餌具有一簇野豬短毛，它讓誘餌在水中移動時可以旋轉，珍珠貝殼移動反射出的光芒
使誘餌看起來向一隻活生生的魚。這件誘餌的尾端是骨頭和耐用的「歐羅納」繩子製成。

Bonito lures include a tuft of boar bristle to make the lure spin as it moved in the water. The light reflected by the movement of the
pearl shell made the lure appear to be a live fish. This lure has a point of bone, and durable line of olonā.

魚誘餌 / 庫克群島的瑪拉希其

Fish lure, Manahiki, Cook Islands

9.5 x 1.5cm

誘餌底部切割上的小小差異，得以辨識它在玻里尼西亞區域內的出處。

Small differences in the cut of a lure's base distinguish it as being from specific localities within Polynesia.

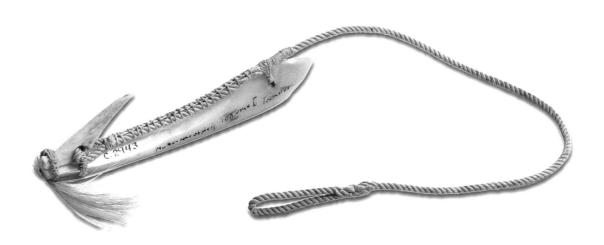

魚誘餌 / 土木土

Fish lure, Tuamotus

11.8 x 1.6cm

來自玻里尼西亞不同地方的鰹魚誘餌有著饒富趣味的相似性。

Bonito lures from different parts of Polynesian bear a striking resemblance.

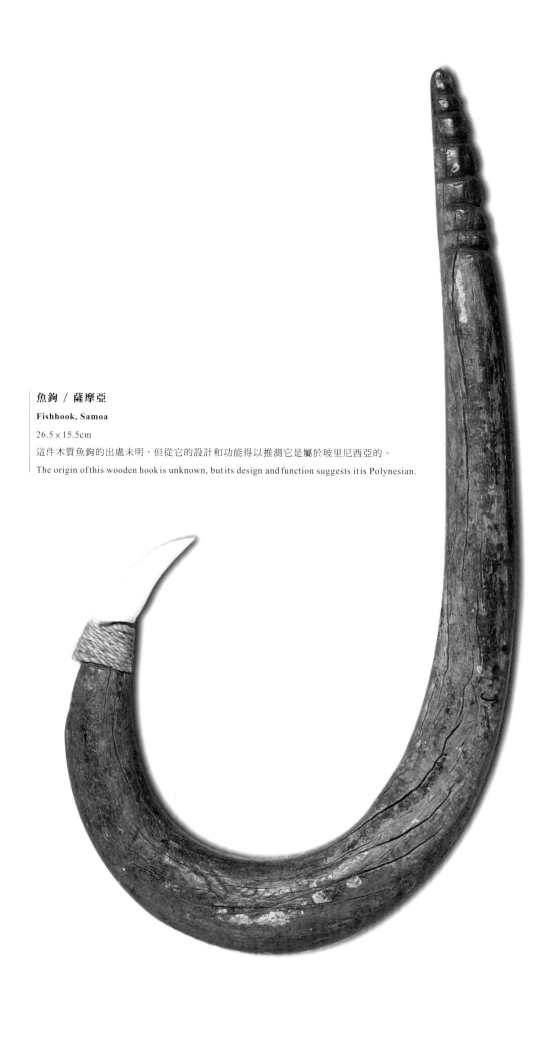

魚鉤 / 薩摩亞

Fishhook, Samoa

26.5 × 15.5cm

這件木質魚鉤的出處未明，但從它的設計和功能得以推測它是屬於玻里尼西亞的。

The origin of this wooden hook is unknown, but its design and function suggests it is Polynesian.

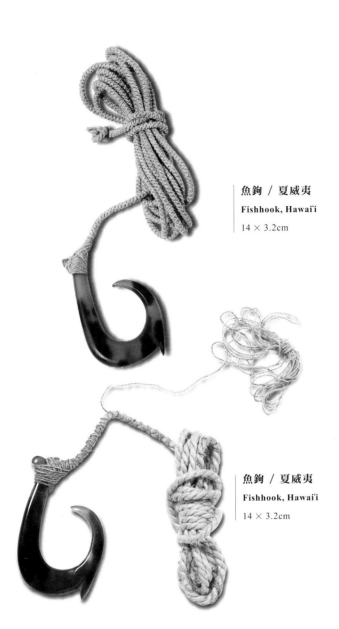

魚鉤 / 夏威夷

Fishhook, Hawaï'i

14 × 3.2cm

魚鉤 / 夏威夷

Fishhook, Hawaï'i

14 × 3.2cm

魚鉤 / 夏威夷

Fishhook, Hawaï'i

5 × 2.5cm

此骨製魚鉤是溫哥華船長的收藏，他在1792年時造訪夏威夷群島。

This bone fishhook was collected by Captain Vancouver who visited the Hawaiian Islands in 1792.

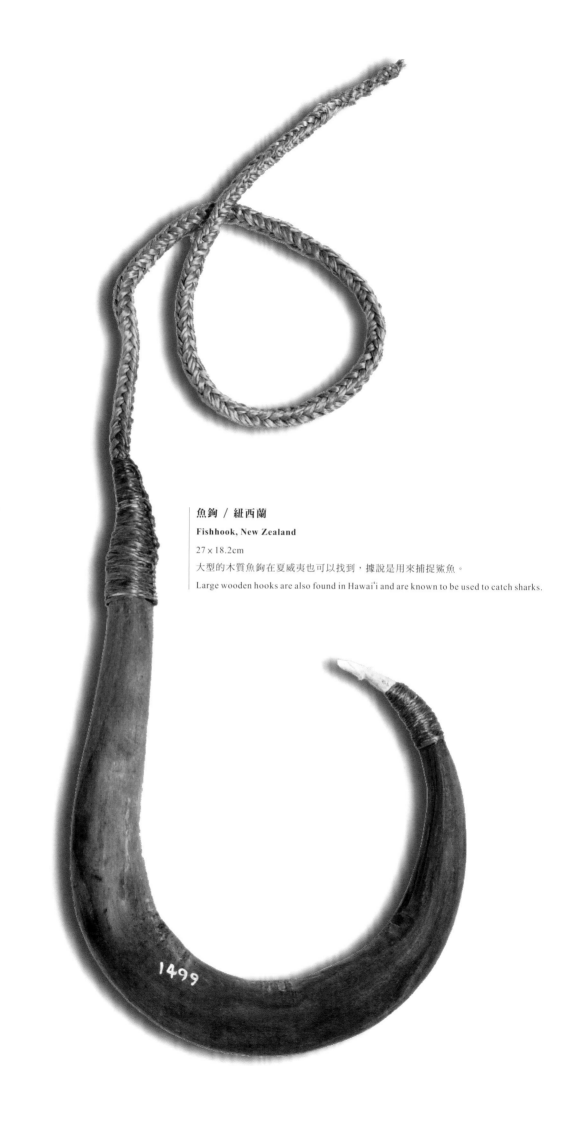

魚鈎 / 紐西蘭

Fishhook, New Zealand

27 × 18.2cm

大型的木質魚鈎在夏威夷也可以找到，據說是用來捕捉鯊魚。

Large wooden hooks are also found in Hawai'i and are known to be used to catch sharks.

魚鉤 / 夏威夷
Fishhook, Hawai`i

9 x 3.6cm

這個組合方式罕見的魚鉤是由兩件骨頭製成，此製造方式讓修理方法變簡單，
每當有需要時，很容易就可以將頂端換新並再度綁在長柄上。

This rare composite fishhook is made of two pieces of bone. Its construction offers a
simple method of repair. The tip can be easily replaced and re-lashed to the shank whenever necessary.

魚鉤 / 紐西蘭
Fishhook, New Zealand

11.5 x 5cm

在此展示的毛利人用的鉤子是由動物骨頭製成。

The Maori hook here is made of animal bone.

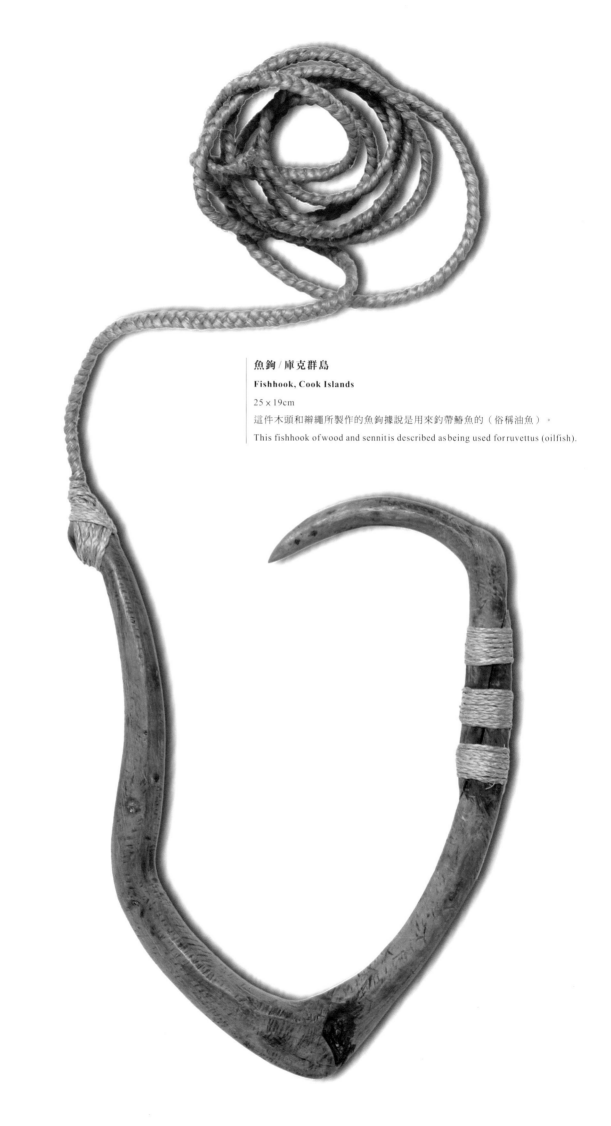

魚鉤 / 庫克群島

Fishhook, Cook Islands

25 × 19cm

這件木頭和辮繩所製作的魚鉤據說是用來釣帶鰆魚的（俗稱油魚）。

This fishhook of wood and sennit is described as being used for ruvettus (oilfish).

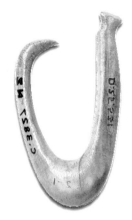

魚鉤 / 紐西蘭

Fishhook, New Zealand

5.4 × 2.9cm

骨頭是製作魚鉤的好材料。

Bone was a good material for fishhooks.

魚鉤 / 復活節島

Fishhook, Rapanui

14 × 10.5cm

此類石製魚鉤是復活節島所使用的。

Stone fishhooks, such as this one, were used in Easter Island.

傳統神祇
Traditional gods

夏威夷人的宗教

宗教信仰遍布在日常生活中的每個層面。夏威夷人心存極大的敬意，來看待大自然與各種自然力量，因為島嶼環境中的這些元素與超自然的存在之間，有著錯綜複雜的關係。許多物體都是「奇諾勞」（*kino lau*，身體形式的神）物體和人類都能擁有一種超自然力量，稱為「瑪那」（*mana*，關於承襲自天神的威信與恩典）。

早期的夏威夷，眾多神祇與半神人影響著所有夏威夷人的作為，夏威夷人最敬重的是四個偉大的神祇：庫（Ku）、卡涅（Kane）、卡那羅亞（Kanaloa）和羅諾（Lono），這是他們與太平洋區的其他文化共同具有的神祇。在「瑪卡希基」期間（*Makahiki*，夏威夷人的豐年祭），人們會給予羅諾特別的獻禮；而在一年的其他時間中，以戰神著稱的庫會受到獻祭與祈求；據說卡那羅亞與卡涅是年輕的冒險家，祂們懷著對刺激探險的渴望來到夏威夷，卡那羅亞管轄海水，卡涅則是淡水的守護者。

個人、家庭神祇以及其他的神，都與特定的職業或特定的地點有關。性靈與人類的領域相結合，兩者是一體的。

大多數的夏威夷神像都由木頭或石頭雕刻而成，在「黑以奧」（*heiau*，神聖的場所或廟宇）發現的神像，可能超過180公分高，至於其他「基夷」（*ki`i*，雕像），特別是那些代表家庭神祇的，就小得多了。

Hawaiian religion

Religious belief pervaded every aspect of daily life. Hawaiians viewed nature and natural forces with great respect, as these elements in the island environment were intricately associated with supernatural beings. Many objects were *kino lau*, body forms of the gods. Both objects and humans could possess a supernatural force called *mana,* associated with the authority and privilege that descended from the gods.

In early Hawai`i, a multitude of gods and demigods guided the actions of all Hawaiians. Hawaiians honored the four great gods shared with other Pacific cultures, Kū, Kane, Kanaloa, and Lono. Special dedication to Lono occurred during the Makahiki period, while Kū, known as the war god, was present and called upon during the remainder of the year. Kanaloa and Kane were thought to have arrived in Hawai`i as young adventures with a lust for exciting exploration. Kanaloa presides over ocean waters and Kane is the patron of fresh water.

Personal and family gods, as well as deities associated with specific occupations, or to a special location abounded. Spiritual and human realms mingled and were one.

Most images of Hawaiian gods were carved from wood or stone. Images found at *heiau*, sacred places or temples, could be well over six feet tall. Many other *ki`i*, carved images, especially those representing family gods were much smaller.

Temple du Roi dans la baie Tir

Lith de Langlumé e de l'Abbaye N.º 4

堤蕊塔堤的羅伊神廟

1816年，路易·科瑞搭乘船長寇茲布的船旅行，記錄了夏威夷島的阿戶耶納·黑以奧。這張圖清楚呈現了西方傳教士
在1820年抵達前，木製宗教雕像的設置方式與如何受到崇敬。

Temple du Roi dans la Baie Tiritatea

Louis Choris, traveling on the ship of Captain von Kotzebue recorded Ahuena Heiau on the Island of Hawai'i in 1816. This illustration
clearly shows how wooden religious images were placed and revered before the arrival of western missionaries in 1820.

夏威夷籃網羽編神像

Baskety figure of Hawaiian god

羽神像

夏威夷人利用精美的羽毛創造出非常特別的物品，對夏威夷來說，獨特的是表面覆以稀有夏威夷鳥類羽毛的神像；其製作方式是以「伊耶伊耶」（`ie`ie）植物的支根編製頭頸部，然後覆蓋細緻的網，再將羽毛束綁在上面。這種神像非常稀有珍貴，據悉全世界現存的只有17件。

籃網羽編神像據說是代表「庫卡伊里摩庫」（Kuka`ilimoku），即卡美哈美哈大帝著名的戰神，此關連是基於在於比夏博物館內發現的一尊與卡美哈美哈歷史有關的羽神像。當時這位年輕戰士從強大的酋長「卡拉尼歐葡悟」（Kalaniopu`u）那裡接受了此著名的羽製「庫卡伊里摩庫」，作為副手的他受酋長任命為其王位繼承者。據說當卡美哈美哈大帝掌權之時，是受到此羽神像的威信所鼓舞支持的。

神像最後裝飾了：珠母貝殼、木栓、和74個環繞著嘴巴的狗牙，紅色「伊伊蜜」（`i`iwi）和黃色「歐歐」（`o`o）羽毛 ，以極小的簇群綁在網狀物上，神像頭頂則是一束束的人類毛髮。

Feathered gods

Hawaiians used exquisite feathers to create items of a very special nature. Unique to Hawaiʻi are basketry images covered with feathers of rare Hawaiian birds. These were made by weaving a head and neck from rootlets of the `ie`ie plant, then covering this with a fine mesh to which bundles of feathers were tied. Such images are very rare, and only seventeen are known to exist throughout the world.

Feathered basketry images are said to represent the god Kūkā`ilimoku, the famous war god of Kamehameha the Great. This association is based on one such image found at Bishop Museum that is linked by history to Kamehameha. The young warrior received the famous feathered Kūkā`ilimoku from the powerful chief Kalaniopu`u, who named him second in succession to his kingdom. It is said that as Kamehameha the Great rose to power, he was encouraged and supported by the authority associated with the feathered Kuka`ilimoku image.

This image is finished with mother-of-pearl shells and wooden pegs to represent eyes, and 74 canine teeth that circle the mouth. What remains of the red `i`iwi and yellow `ō`ō feathers are found in tiny clusters tied to the netting. Crowning the image are tufts of human hair.

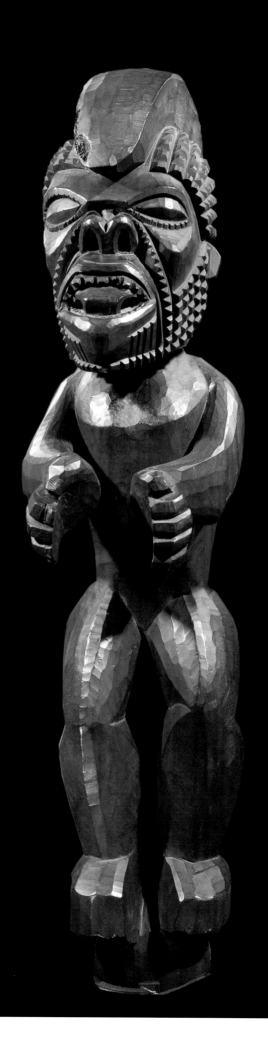

1825年五月，英國海軍艦隊金髮尤物號的指揮官拜倫爵士帶著卡美哈美哈二世及其
夫人卡瑪瑪祿的遺體抵達夏威夷，兩人在拜訪倫敦時死於麻疹，拜倫和他的船員們
受邀拜訪名為「哈雷歐科阿威」的酋長聖地。卡拉尼摩庫酋長准予這些人拿走任何
想要的珍品。據信，此遠征隊的自然學家安德魯‧布魯珊接受了數件物品，它們被
保留在其家人之手將近一個世紀。1924年，這座布魯珊神像回到夏威夷，贈與比夏
博物館。

In May 1825, Lord Byron, commander of the H.M.S. Blonde, arrived in Hawaiʻi with the
bodies of Kamehameha II and his wife, Kamāmalu. Both had died of measles during a visit
to London. Byron and his crew were invited to visit the once sacred site of the chiefs known
as Hale-o-Keawe. The men were granted permission by Chief Kalanimoku to take "any
curiosity" they desired. It is believe that the expedition naturalist, Andrew Bloxam,
received several items which remained with his family for nearly a century. The
Bloxam image returned to Hawaiʻi and was given to the Bishop Museum in 1924.

夏威夷木神像，布魯珊神像
H133 × 27 × 34cm
比夏博物館原件的複製品
Hawaiian wooden image, Bloxam Image
Replica of original at Bishop Museum

「外阿奴耶奴耶」的字面意思是「水中之虹」，原件在1896年時發現於考艾島的沼澤地，透過口傳傳說，這個平版形雕像被認定為此水域之神。然而，關於祂的重要性所知甚少。

The original Waiānuenue（literally Water-rainbow）was found in swampy land in 1896 on the Island of Kauaʻi. Through oral tradition, the slab-type image was identified as this water deity, though little is known about his significance.

夏威夷木神像，外阿奴耶奴耶
H160 × 49 × 29cm
比夏博物館原件的複製品
Hawaiian wooden image, Waiānuenue
Replica of original at Bishop Museum

庫卡伊里摩庫（「庫」）最常被認定為卡美哈美哈大帝的戰神，祂對農耕與日常生活的其他層面具有極大影響，這件比夏博物館著名庫神像的複製品，是1964年為前往紐約萬國博覽會所製作的，它相當近似目前陳列於夏威夷的原始神像。

原始的神像是由來到夏威夷的基督教傳教士們所收藏，其影響力造成了當時夏威夷宗教、社會結構和生活形態的急遽改變。在1830年代前，僅在傳教士抵達之後的十年，傳統的夏威夷神像即被視為珍品蒐藏，或因夏威夷原住民擔心它們遭到破壞而加以藏匿。

在夏威夷境外的兩尊神像，幾乎和比夏博物館內的這個一模一樣。這件複製品所依據的雕像是在1895年時從美國海外宣道會的手中購買的。

Kūkā`ilimoku ("Kū") was most often recognized as the war god of Kamehameha the Great, the he had great influence in agriculture and other aspects of daily life. This replica of the famous Kū image at Bishop Museum was created in 1964 for travel to the New York World's Fair. It closely replicates the original *kii* (image) now display in Hawaï i.

The original image was collected by missionaries to Hawaï i at a time when their influence caused dramatic change in Hawaiian religion, social structure, and lifestyles. By the 1830s, barely a decade after the arrival of Christian missionaries, traditional Hawaiian images were being collected as curiosities, or hidden away by native Hawaiians who feared their destruction.

Two images almost identical to the one at Bishop Museum exist in museums outside of Hawaï i. The *kii* upon which this replica was based was purchased from the American Board of Commissions for Foreign Missions in 1895.

夏威夷木神像，「庫卡伊里摩庫」 (*Kūkā`ilimoku*)
H220 × 65 × 46cm
比夏博物館原件的複製品
Hawaiian wooden image, *Kūkā`ilimoku*
Replica of original at Bishop Museum

夏威夷的文化寶藏
Treasures created by early Hawaiian

檀香山王宮內，慶祝Kalakaua國王50歲大壽的 *Hookupu* (禮物)
Hookupu (gifts) for King Kalakaua's 50th birthday in the Throne Room of Iola

「那‧米亞‧瑪卡麥」（Na Mea Makamae）

早期夏威夷人所創造的許多珍寶，見證了傳統工匠和藝術家的精湛技藝。島嶼環境只提供了有限的資源，然而夏威夷人所製作的工具、衣物、持家的用具和祭典肖像等，全都需要技術、精確性與無私的奉獻。

這些「米亞‧瑪卡麥」（*mea makamae*，高價值的東西）是由簡單的材料製成的：石頭、木頭、植株的某些部位、羽毛、貝殼、牙齒和骨頭等，每一樣創作物都具有實用性、功能性以及獨特的美感。

昔日的夏威夷匠師們發展出一套卓越的標準，今日的藝術家藉由研究這些文物，得以揭露傳統技藝的奧秘，然後，將此遺產傳給未來的世代。

Na Mea Makamae

Treasures created by early Hawaiian attest to the mastery of traditional crafters and artists. The island setting offered only limited resources, yet Hawaiians produced tools, clothing, household items and ceremonial figures that required skill, precision and unstinted dedication.

Such *mea makamae*, things of great value, were made from simple materials : stone, wood, plant parts, feathers, shell, teeth, and bone. Each creation had utility and function, as well as unique beauty.

Hawaiian masters developed a standard of excellence. By studying these artifacts, today's artists are able to uncover the secrets of traditional skills and, in turn, pass on this legacy to future generations.

Ioane (右) 和家人在吃芋泥

Ioane (rt.) and family eating poi

木缽和木盤

「烏美柯耶・拉奧」（`Umeke lā`au，木缽）的尺寸有可能是大型的，用以裝盛群體食用的芋泥；或是小型的，裝盛個人用的食物。美麗的夏威夷木製容器的製造，運用了最高的技術。最早期的缽，以石器與打磨器經手工製作而成，傳統的最後修整方式巧妙地運用石栗（kukui）堅果油，讓缽覆上一層輕柔的光澤。十九世紀時，蟲膠盛行，它被用來取代傳統的修整方法，使得容器有了明亮閃耀的新面貌。

芋泥板，厚重並具有耐用的表面，將芋頭放在其上，磨成泥狀，以製作夏威夷人的主食。

Wood bowls and platters

`Umeke lā`au

The highest skill was applied to the manufacture of beautiful Hawaiian wooden containers. `Umeke lā`au, wooden bowls, could be large and used for a communal serving of poi, or of a smaller size to hold an individual serving. The earliest bowls were made by hand, and with the use of stone tools and polishers. The traditional finish was a fine application of kukui nut oil that clothed the bowl with a soft luster. Shellac became popular in the 19th century, and was used to replace the traditional finish with a bright and shiny new look.

Poi boards, upon which taro root was mashed into poi, were thick and heavy- made to provide a sturdy surface for the production of the Hawaiian staple food.

芋泥缽
`Umeke poi kou, poi bowl

H18 × Dia20 cm

這件少有的缽具有不規則邊緣,這使得它成為一件特別的作品。

This unusual bowl has an irregular rim, marking it as a special piece.

木缽
`Umeke lä`au, wooden bowl

H11 × Dia23 cm

此缽呈現角度的面使它成為一件獨特、美麗的作品。

The angular faces of this bowl make it stand out as a unique and beautiful piece.

個人用的碗
`Umeke mäna`ai, single serving bowl

H9.5 × Dia14 cm

這個小碗屬於個人使用,曾經用來供小孩子首次食用固體食物,
為卡美哈美哈四世的夫人愛瑪王后所有。

This small bowl, a single serving bowl thought to have been used for a child's first solid meal,
was owned by Queen Emma, wife of Kamehameha IV.

木鉢

`Umeke la`au, wooden bowl

H22 × Dia17 cm

最初的木製食鉢是由「寇烏」木（橙花破布子，*Cordia subcordata*）所製。

Wooden foodbowls were primarily made from *kou (Cordia subcordata)* wood.

芋泥缽

'Umeke poi, poi bowl

H27 × Dia31 cm

用來強化或修復木頭上的裂紋的補丁片，讓缽的表面具有動人的圖樣，
夏威夷缽的修復包含蝴蝶修補法、縫法、填補法和栓釘法。

Patches to strengthen or repair flaws in the wood create an appealing pattern in the walls of the bowl.

Hawaiian bowl repairs include butterfly mends, stitching, fills, and pegging.

小型芋泥板

Papa ku`i `ai, small poi board

L88 × W42 cm

煮過的芋頭放在沈重的木製芋泥板上擣製成糊狀，有時候男人們會一起製作，這種場合所用的板子是相當大的。
這個小型板適合個人用來製作芋泥。

Cooked taro was pounded into a paste on a heavy wooden poi board. Men sometimes worked together and the boards used for these occasions were quite large.
This small board is fitting for a single poi maker.

椰子

椰子樹的果實（*niu*，尼梧），有時被製成杯子或菸葉容器。
椰子高腳杯在十九世紀末流行起來，稍後，在二十世紀初，
這些高腳杯與椰子製器皿變成觀光客流行的收藏品。

Coconut

Niu

The nuts of coconut palms (*niu*) were sometimes made into cups or tobacco containers. The coconut goblets became popular toward the end of the 19th century. Later during the early 1900s, such goblets and coconut dishes became popular collectibles for visiting tourists.

高腳杯

coconut goblets

H13.5 × Dia14cm

椰子的纖維供予早期的夏威夷人製作繩索，果實也是食物、飲品的來源，葉子可以用在家中，
然而，像這樣的椰子杯組一直到19世紀晚期才有。

Coconuts provided early Hawaiians with fiber to make cordage. The nuts contained a source of food and drink, and the leaves had household uses. However, coconut-serving sets like this were not made until the late 19th century.

阿瓦杯

Olo awa, ʻawa cups

L19 × W10.5 × H7cm

阿瓦杯

Olo awa, ʻawa cups

L17 × W15 × H8cm

阿瓦杯

Olo awa, ʻawa cups

椰子殼所製造的杯子可以當作小型的研缽來使用，或者裝盛「阿瓦」－「卡瓦」（ *Piper methysticum*，卡瓦胡椒）的根所製造的一種鎮靜、迷醉性飲品。

阿瓦杯的製作是把椰子殼縱寬面剖開，這種切割法指出了使用者的階級，這種杯子最有可能是「卡戶納」－夏威夷的神職人員－所使用。

Cups made from coconut shell could be used as small mortars, or to serve awa, a narcotic drink made from the root of kawa *(Piper methysticum)*. Awa cups were made by cutting a coconut shell lengthwise. The kind of cut designated the class of user; these cups were most likely used by *kahuna*, or Hawaiian priests.

菸葉容器
Hano baka, tobacco containers

L12.4 × W5cm

菸葉容器
Hano baka, tobacco containers

L8.6 × W9cm

在庫克船長和其他外國人到來之前，夏威夷人是不知道菸葉的，抽煙很快就變成一種流行趨勢，這裡的這類菸葉容器是早期對於此流行的回應。

Tobacco was unknown to Hawaiians until the arrival of Captain Cook and other foreigners. Smoking quickly became fashionable and tobacco containers, such as these, were early responses to the fad.

煙斗

***Ipu baka*, tobacco pipe**

88 × 42cm

這件少見的煙斗具有兩個頭，它為住在夏威夷島的一位老巫師所擁有。

The unusual double-bowl pipe belonged to an old sorcerer on the Island of Hawai`i.

在 *hale pili*（茅草屋）旁搗製芋泥的夏威夷男子們
Hawaiian men pounding poi beside *hale pili* (grass house)

石器

「坡哈庫」

與西方人接觸之前，夏威夷島上無法取得金屬，因此早期夏威夷人廣泛運用「坡哈庫」（pōhaku，石頭），製造耐用的日常用具。

除了某些「坡哈庫」是以其自然形態而被運用以外，其他大部分都是因應特定用途而塑形的。由於夏威夷人只能運用其他石頭做切割，來將原石製成用具，因此這是一項辛苦的工作。

Stone implements

Pōhaku

Because metal was not available in the Hawaiian Islands until after western contact, early Hawaiians made extensive use of *pōhaku* (stone) to produce hardy, everyday tools. Some *pōhaku* were used in the natural forms, but most were shaped to serve a specific purpose. This was a difficult task since Hawaiians only had other stones to cut and finish raw stone into implements.

玄武岩石錛

***Ko`i,* adze (basalt)**

L32.3 × W7 × T6cm

老練的工匠細心的挑選石頭，鑿出雛形後，再將錛磨成形。最優秀的製錛者能夠製造出堅固耐用，
同時又具有美感的錛。

Expert craftsmen carefully chose their stone, chipped out a rough form, and ground the adze into shape.

The best adze makers could create *ko`i* that were strong and durable, and with an aesthetic quality.

玄武岩石錛

***Ko`i,* adze (basalt)**

L7 × W2 × T4cm

錛的頭通常會裝上木柄，再細心地用椰繩綑綁就完成了。
不過，據說某些小型錛沒有裝柄就直接使用了。

Adze heads were often hafted to wooden handles, carefully lashed with coconut cordage to finish the tool.

However, it is thought that some of the smaller adze heads were used without handles.

玄武岩石錛

Ko`i, adze (basalt)

L27 × W8 × T4cm

尺寸、形狀多變化，顯示這些切割器具的不同用途及功能。

The variety of sizes and shapes indicate a range of purposes and uses for these cutting implements.

錘
Sinker
L6 × W5 × T4.5cm

錘
Sinker
L7 × W5 × T5cm

錘
Sinker
L10 × W6 × T3cm

此類的玄武岩石錘，讓吸引章魚的貝殼誘餌有了重量。

Basalt sinkers, such as this one, provide the weight for shell lures that attracted octopus.

章魚誘餌

Luhe`e, **octopus lure**

L21 × W7.5 × T12cm

夏威夷的章魚誘餌和玻里尼西亞其他地方的類似。它運用石頭的重量讓餌（寶螺殼）繫在一支樹枝上下沈，漁夫手握住線，期望誘餌能夠吸引體積夠大的獵物，繩子的輕微拉動表示章魚已經進入了陷阱，此時漁夫會快速地拉繩子，把捕獲物拉上來。

The Hawaiian octopus lure is similar to others in Polynesia. Stone weights are used to sink the "bait" cowry shells attached to a piece of branch. The fisherman held the line hoping that his lure would attract a sizable prey. A gentle pull on the cord would signal that an octopus had settled on the trap, and the fisherman would quickly tug at the line and pull up the catch.

玄武岩石杵

Pohaku ku`i `ai, **pounder (basalt)**

H19 × Dia14cm (at base)

在夏威夷群島的大部分地方，製作芋泥都被認為是男人的本分，許多博物館收藏的杵都很沈重，
且供單手握持。杵的製作需符合個人的抓握以及對重量與形狀的偏好。

On most of the Hawaiian Islands, the making of poi was thought to be duty of males. Many of the pounders in museum collections are heavy

and meant to held by one hand. Pounders are made to fit the individual grip and preference in weight and shape.

玄武岩石杵

Pohaku ku`i `ai, **pounder (basalt)**

H14 × W13cm × T8cm

此類環狀杵是北方島－考艾、尼豪－所特有。這類杵似乎是供一雙小手使用的，
使用時也許比較是常用於擠壓，而非搗搥。

"Ring" pounders such as this one are typically associated with the northern islands of Kaua`i and Ni`ihau.

These seem to be implements used by a pair of smaller hands, perhaps more to mash than to pound.

投石器的石頭
`Alā o kama`a, slingstones
L8 × W4.5cm

投石器的石頭
`Alā o kama`a, slingstones
L6.5 × W5cm

石頭和椰繩製作的投石器在交戰時是很有用的，這通常是女性使用的武器。

Stones and slings made of coconut cordage were effective in warfare, often being weapons used by females.

鉢
Poho pōhaku, **bowls**
H5 × Dia9.5cm

鉢
Poho pōhaku, **bowls**
H6 × Dia7.5cm

適合一個手掌握持的小鉢，可以用來放裝飾樹皮衣的染料、混合釣魚用的魚餌，或研磨烹調用的香料。據說「卡戶納」
（專門的術士或神職人員）曾經用過這些玄武岩石鉢。

Small bowls that fit the palm of a hand could be used to hold the dye for decorating backcloth, to mix fishing bait, or to grind flavoring for food. *Kahuna,* specialized practitioners or priests, are said to have used these basalt bowls.

玄武岩鏡
Kilo pōhaku, basalt mirrors
Dia21.3cm

高度打磨過的玄武岩，因顏色深才挑選它。以它為背景，前面包覆一層薄薄水層的表面來作為鏡子。
夏威夷人珍視玄武岩鏡。

Highly polished basalt, chosen for its dark color, becomes the background for the reflective surface crated with a thin layer of water.
Hawaiians treasured basalt mirrors.

玄武岩鏡

Kilo pōhaku, **basalt mirrors**

Dia13.7cm

搬運葫蘆的夏威夷人（彩色明信片）
Hawaiian man calabash carrier, Hawai'i. Color postcard.

葫蘆製容器

水壺稱為「惠‧弗艾」（hue wai），目前
發現的有許多不同的形狀與尺寸，這些以
「夷蒲」（ipu，葫蘆）製造的容器有時候
會飾以「帕魏黑」的圖樣（pāwehe，幾何圖
樣），它們和尼豪島有關連。

「烏美柯耶‧坡惠」（`Umeke pōhue，葫
蘆食缽）加入木缽的行列，被用來儲存與
裝盛食物。「坡惠」（Pōhue）是泛指爬
藤類植物的一般用語，夏威夷人廣植葫蘆
藤，主要是扁蒲（Lagenaria siceraria）。
就像水壺一樣，某些葫蘆缽也被飾以線型
圖樣，此類線型圖樣稱為「烏美柯耶‧帕
魏黑」（`umeke pāwehe）。

Gourd containers

Water bottles, called *hue wai*, are found in
many shapes and sizes. These containers of
gourd, or *ipu*, were sometimes decorated with
geometric patterns called *pāwehe*, and these
were associated with the island of Ni`ihau.
`Umeke pōhue, gourd food bowls, added to
the supply of wooden bowls used to store and
serve food. *Pōhue* was a general term for
plants with creeping vines, and Hawaiian
extensively cultivated gourd plants (mostly
Lagenaria siceraria). Like *hue wai*, some
gourd bowls were decorated with linear
patterns; these were called *`umeke pāwehe*.

夏威夷男子擣製芋泥
Hawaiian man pounding poi

装飾水器的幾何圖樣，其製作方法並沒有被確切了解，現代的再製品仍舊缺乏早期物品的光澤與美感。

葫蘆水瓶

Hue wai, gourd water bottle

H36 × Dia23cm

裝飾水器的幾何圖樣，其製作方法並沒有被確切了解，現代的再製品仍舊缺乏早期物品的光澤與美感。

The method of creating the geometric patterns that adorn this water holder is not understood with certainty.

Modern re-creations still lack the luster and beauty of the early examples.

葫蘆水瓶

Hue wai, gourd water bottle

H34 × Dia30cm

這個葫蘆容器所裝飾的幾何圖樣，類似用來握持此類容器的提繩。

This *hue wai* is decorated with geometric patterns that resemble the cord carrier used to hold such containers.

飾紋葫蘆

`*Umeke pāwehe*, decorated gourd

H19 × Dia22cm (at widest)

要作為裝盛小物品的缽、隔濾器和容器來使用時，葫蘆比木頭更好。

Gourd preceded wood in its use as bowls, strainers and containers for small items.

附椰子提繩的葫蘆容器

`*Umeke pohue*, gourd bowl with coconut carrier

H26.4 × Dia17.5cm

這件水瓶有一個長牙製的瓶塞。

This water bottle includes a stopper made of ivory.

樹皮布的製作

夏威夷的布料

「卡帕」（*Kapa*，夏威夷樹皮布）的製作，傳統上是委派給女人的工作，構樹（paper mulberry，學名：*Brossonetia papyrifera*）內層的樹皮被稱為「哇烏柯耶」（*wauke*），經常被用來製作「卡帕」。在木砧板上，以敲打器具敲打平整，直到紙一般的厚度，敲打的最後幾個階段，會使用具有圖紋的敲打工具，因而會造成一種細微的、浮水印般的裝飾。乾燥後，可在樹皮布上繪畫、版印，或以額外的圖樣壓印。

Making kapa

Hawaiian fabric

The making of *kapa*, Hawaiian bark cloth, is a task traditionally delegated to women. The inner bark of the paper mulberry tree, called *wauke* (*Brossonetia papyrifera*) , is often used to make *kapa*. It is flattened to paper-fine thickness with beaters upon a wood anvil. A patterned beater was used in the final stages of beating, and this produced a subtle, watermark decoration. After drying, the *kapa* could be painted, stenciled or stamped with additional patterns.

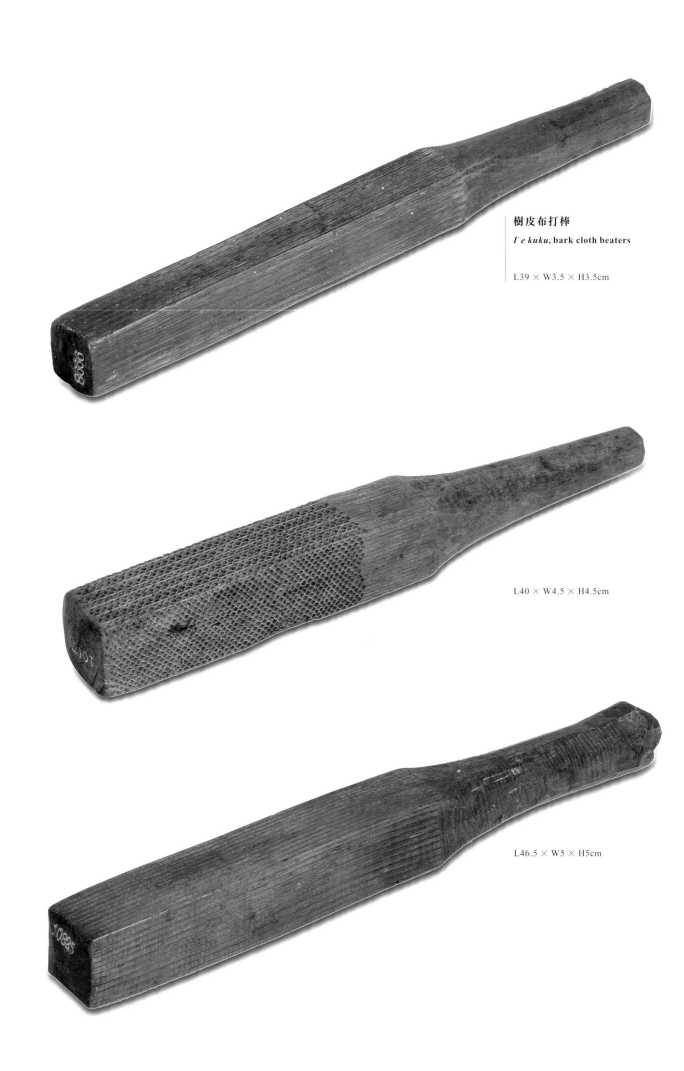

樹皮布打棒

I`e kuku, bark cloth beaters

L39 × W3.5 × H3.5cm

L40 × W4.5 × H4.5cm

L46.5 × W5 × H5cm

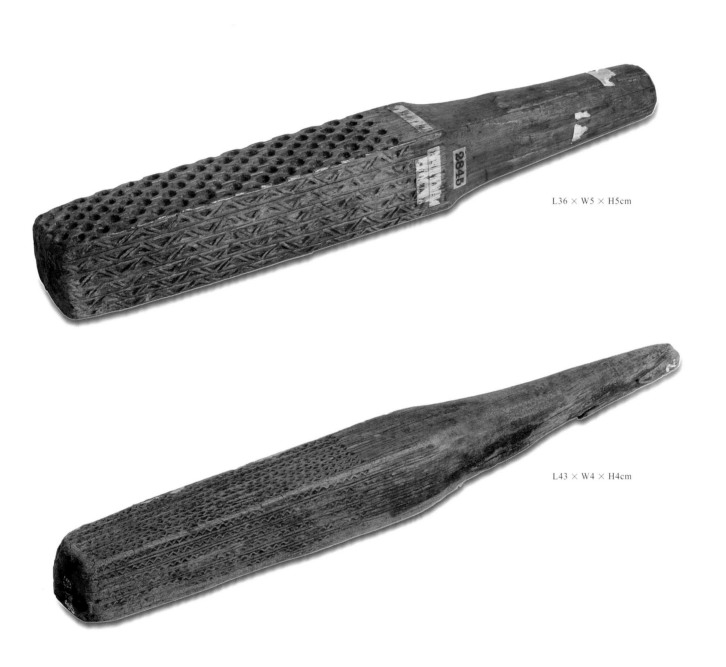

L36 × W5 × H5cm

L43 × W4 × H4cm

這些樹皮布打棒展現了圖樣的變化類型，在製作卡帕的最後幾個階段時供壓印。
These bark cloth beaters show the range of patterns for imprinting during the final stages of making *kapa*.

竹製印模

`Ohe kāpala, bamboo stamps

less than L42 × W1.5cm

樹皮布的畫線器

Lapa, kapa liners

竹製的畫線器和印模被用來裝飾做好的樹皮布。

Liners and stamps made of bamboo were used to decorate finished pieces of bark cloth.

less than L45 × W5cm

溝槽器

Grooving implement

L32 × W7cm

溝槽組有時候是用來讓樹皮布製作的「瑪樓」（纏腰布）和「帕梧」（裙子）具有特殊的修飾紋。

「帕帕侯雷庫阿烏拉」上的細緻線條是以鯊魚牙齒精確地製造的。

Grooving sets were sometimes used to give a special finish *malo* (loincloths) and *pa`u* (skirts), items of clothing made from bark cloth.

The fine lines in the *papa hole kua`ula* were precisely made with sharks' teeth.

樹皮布溝槽板
Papa hole kua`ula, grooved *kapa* board
L82 × W21 × H1cm

缽和染料
Bowl and dye
H2.5 × Dia13cm

林投刷
Pandanus brush
L6cm

天然材料製成的染料和簡單的刷子也都是用來裝飾樹皮布的。

Dyes made from natural materials and simple brushes were also used to decorate *kapa*.

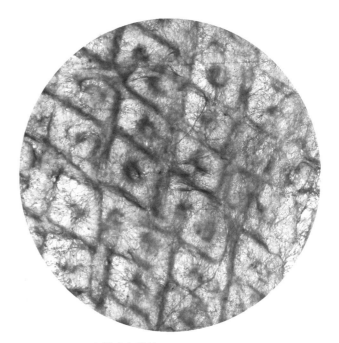

樹皮布樣品

Kapa samples

55 × 42cm

夏威夷樹皮布的製作的典型的特色是
纖維的製作過程的延長,以便讓織品
變得耐用、細緻,以及廣泛的裝飾技
法和顏色。

Typical features of Hawaiian bark cloth
making are the extensive processing of
the fiber to create a sturdy and fine
fabric and the broad range of decoration
technique and color.

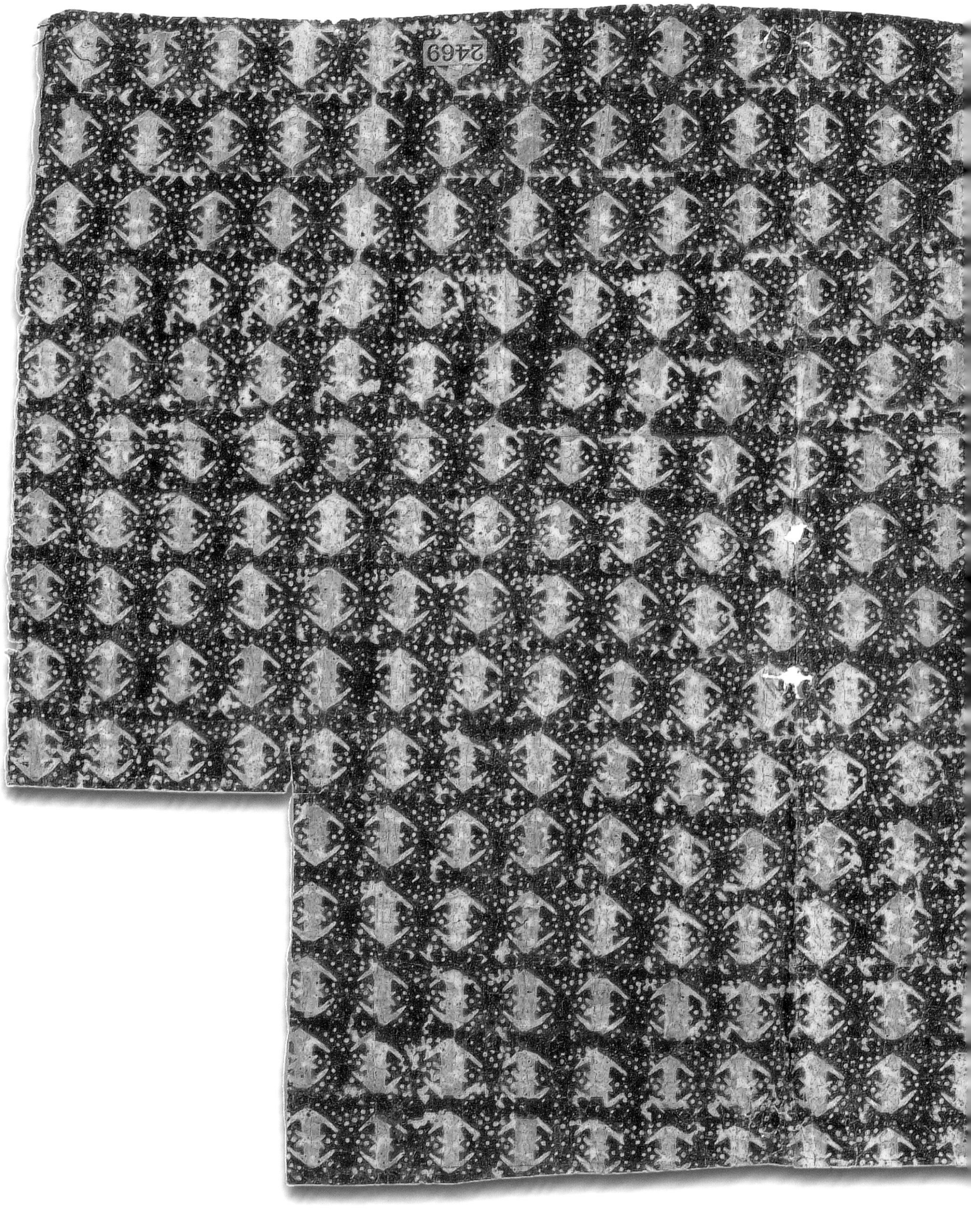
2469

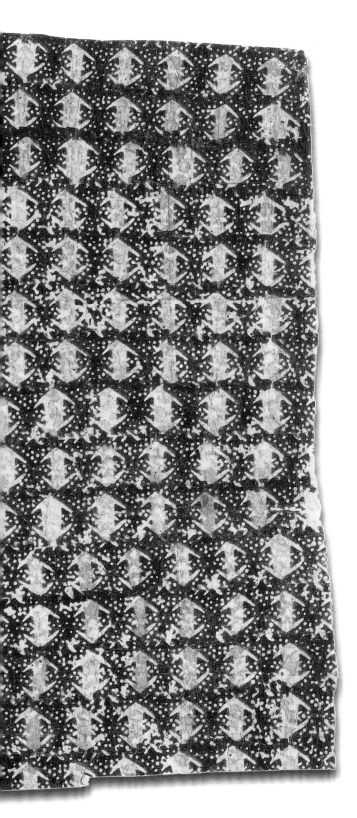

樹皮布樣品

Kapa samples

L58.5 × W42cm

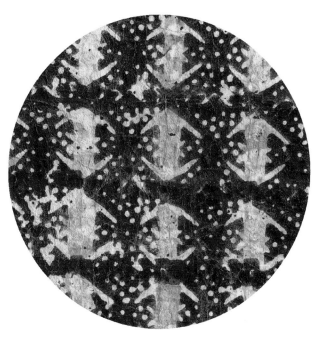

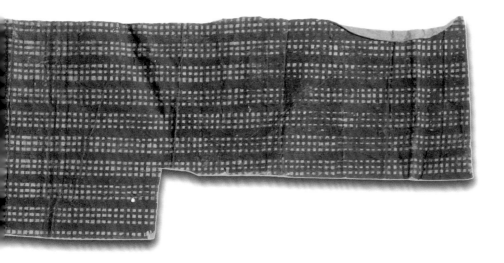

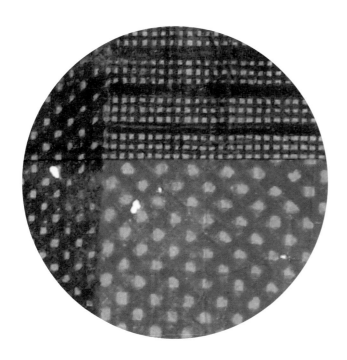

樹皮布樣品

Kapa samples

L59 × W34cm

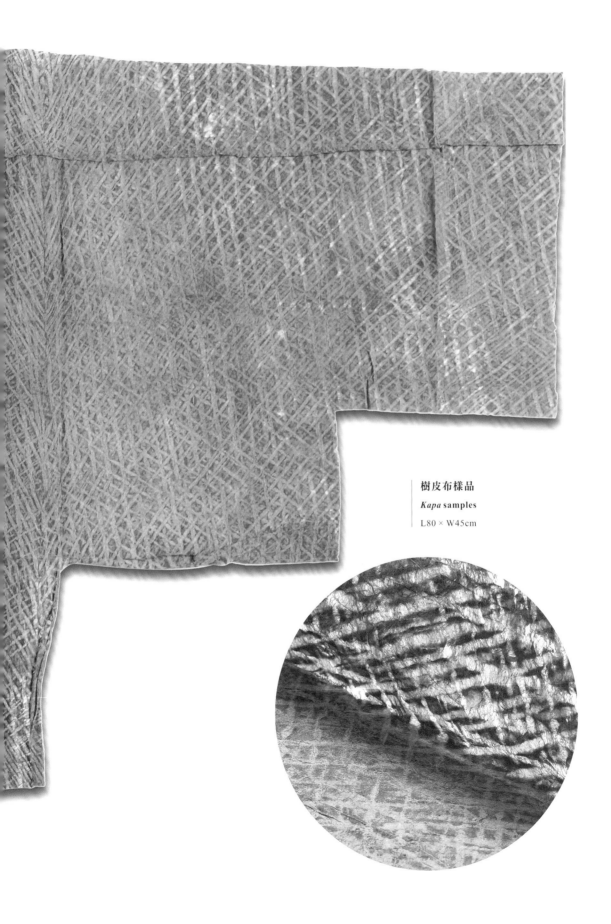

樹皮布樣品
Kapa samples
L80 × W45cm

編織林投蓆

Kihaa Piilani weaving lauhala mat

紡織、編織

織物

大部分的織物都由「勞・哈拉」（*lau hala*，林投樹的葉子）製成。樹葉收割以後會加熱處理，使其凋萎，並呈現一種淡淡的色彩。去除葉脈與尾端，然後在太陽底下曬乾，經過重擊之後，使葉子變得柔軟，然後視需要的寬度將它撕開。運用「勞・哈拉」製作的有：蓆子、袋子、扇子、帽子及其他物品。

尼豪島和考艾島的匠師們，運用輪傘莎草（稱做 *makaloa*，瑪卡洛阿，學名：*Cyperus laeviatus*）創造最精美的睡蓆。儘管這種植物也生長在太平洋的其他地區，但是，只有夏威夷人運用此薄長狀的蘆桿，製作出兼具驚人美感與耐用性的蓆子。

Weaving and plaiting

Woven goods

Most woven items were made from the leaves of the pandanus tree, called *lau hala*. The leaves were harvested and treated with heat to wilt them and to obtain a lighter color. Their spines and ends were removed, and then they were dried in the sun. The leaves were pounded to make them supple, and split to the required width. Mats, bags, fans, hats and other items were made from *lau hala*.

Masters from the islands of Ni`ihau and Kaua`i created the finest of Hawaiian sleeping mats from sedge called *makaloa* (*Cyperus laeviatus*). Though the plant grows elsewhere in the Pacific, Hawaiians are the only people to use the thin, long reeds to make mats of incredible beauty and durability.

蓆子

Moena, mat

L142 × W67cm

這件林投蓆的精美編織使得它與眾不同。

The fine weave of this *lau hala* mat sample makes it unusual.

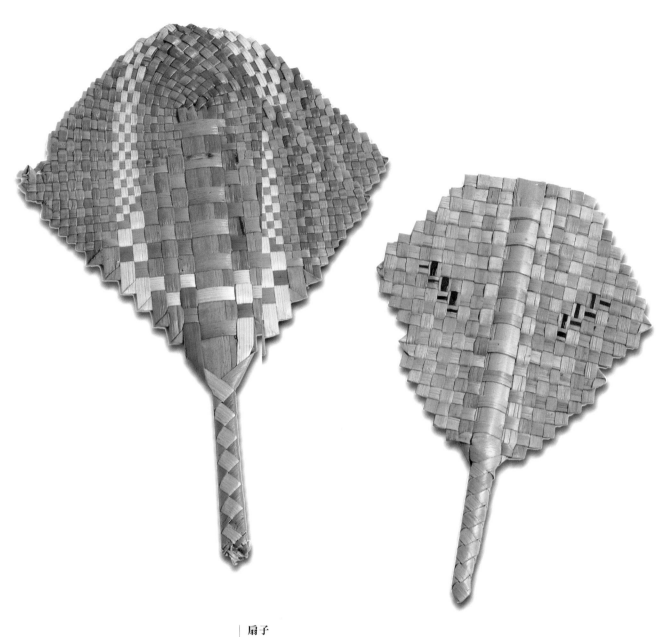

扇子

Pe`ahi, **fans**

林投扇的製作容易，至今仍然很普及。

Lau hala fans are simple to make and still very popular today.

帽子

Pāpale, hat

L30 × W36 × H10.5cm

帽子是西方人抵達群島後才引進的，然而，夏威夷的匠師很快就發展出利用林投葉和其他植物材料製作帽子的技術。
Hats were introduced at the arrival of West to the Islands, but Hawaiian craftsman quickly developed the skill of hat making with *lau hala* and other plant materials.

瑪卡洛阿草蓆

Moena makaloa, makaloa mat

L56 × W44cm

重要的酋長所使用的蓆子是由瑪卡洛阿莎草（輪傘莎草）所製，這種草蓆的編製和編圖樣都是需要技術、耐心和計畫的，圖樣和式樣通常都是有命名的，在此展示的這個稱為「帕帕烏拉」。

Mats for prominent chiefs were made from the sedge *makaloa (Cyperus laevigatus)*. The plaiting and patterning of such mats demanded skill, patience and planning. Pattern and motifs were usually named; the one demonstrated here is known as *papaʻula*.

F.W.Frohawk, del. et. lith.
West, Newman, imp.

VESTIARIA COCCINEA.

伊伊蜜鳥

ʻIiwi *Vestiaria coccinea*

羽毛工藝

「阿里夷」（*ali`i*，夏威夷的酋長）穿著的華貴羽毛服裝，大多以幾種挑選出來的森林鳥類的羽毛製成。現存的傳統羽製標本，清楚證實了夏威夷人的藝術水準與美感是高超絕倫的，這些衣物包含：披風、斗蓬、帽子與花環。製作此類羽製珍寶時，每一個工作環節都需要小心留意，而且作工要精細。最後的完成工作，只能成於具有絕佳技術的專家之手。這些傑出的作品都是供「阿里夷」使用，因此這樣的細心製作是合乎需要的。

Feather work

Ali`i, Hawaiian chiefs, wore magnificent feather garments, most often made with feathers of a few select forest birds. Existing examples of traditional feather work give clear evidence of the advanced degree of Hawaiian artistry and aesthetics. Garments included capes, cloaks, helmets, and lei. Each task in the production of these feathered treasures required careful attention and meticulous handwork, and was accomplished only by specialists with considerable skill. It was fitting that these masterpieces were reserved for *ali`i.*

羽毛披風

`Ahu`ula, feather cape

L82 × W59cm

製作此件羽毛披風所使用的是「伊伊蜜」鳥的紅色羽
毛和「歐歐」鳥的黃色羽毛，羽毛收集後，五六支一
小簇，再以「歐羅納」做成的細繩綁緊，然後再把這
些小撮的羽毛束綁在歐羅納繩所製的編網上。

這件披風是早期的美國傳教士所收藏，他在1820年就
到夏威夷了。

The red feathers of the *`i`wi*, and the yellow feathers of the
`ō`ō were used to make this feather cape. Feathers were
collected and prepared in small bundles of five or six and
secured with a thin cord of *olonā*. The bundles were then
tied a netting of *olonā* cordage.

This cape was collected by early American missionaries
who arrived in Hawai`i beginning in 1820.

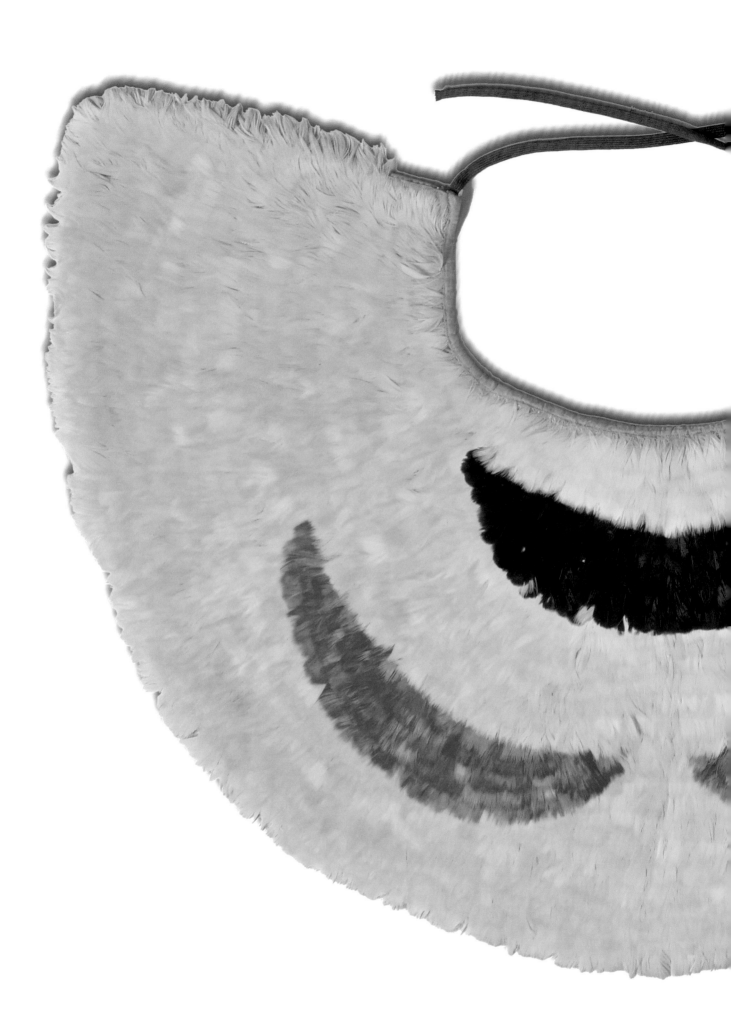

羽毛披風
`Ahu`ula, feather cape

L76 × W46cm

1800年代晚期，許多羽毛被拿來製作羽製服裝
的鳥類已經變得稀少，因此在製作「傳統」的
披風時，用了進口的染色羽毛以及布質裡襯。
這件披風是卡琵歐拉妮王后在1883年為了卡拉
卡瓦國王的加冕慶典所訂製的其中一件。

By the late 1800s, many of the birds whose feathers
were used for feather garments were rare. Dyed
feathers were imported and fabric backing was used
in making "traditional" capes. This cape is one of
several ordered by Queen Kapi`olani for ceremonies
celebrating the coronation of King Kalākaua in 1883.

羽毛樣本
Feather Samples

羽毛樣本

熟練的匠師細心準備製作斗蓬與披風用的羽毛。羽毛收集後,加以仔細清潔,再以歐羅納細繩綁成一束束。

「阿戶烏拉」的製作準備工作,依據羽毛大小與顏色加以選擇,然後以極細緻的繩子將五六支做成一束,之後,將這些羽毛束綁在堅韌的歐羅納繩製成的編網上。這種工作非常辛苦,但羽製品的成果則是美麗。

Feather samples

Feathers used to make cloaks and capes were carefully prepared by skilled masters. Once collected, the feathers were carefully cleaned and bundled with thin cords of *olonā*.

In preparation for the making of an *'ahu 'ula,* feathers were selected according to size and color, and then bound in a cluster of five or six. A very fine cord was used for this. The bundles were then tied into a netting of strong *olonā* cordage. The work was painstaking, but the resulting feather piece was beautiful.

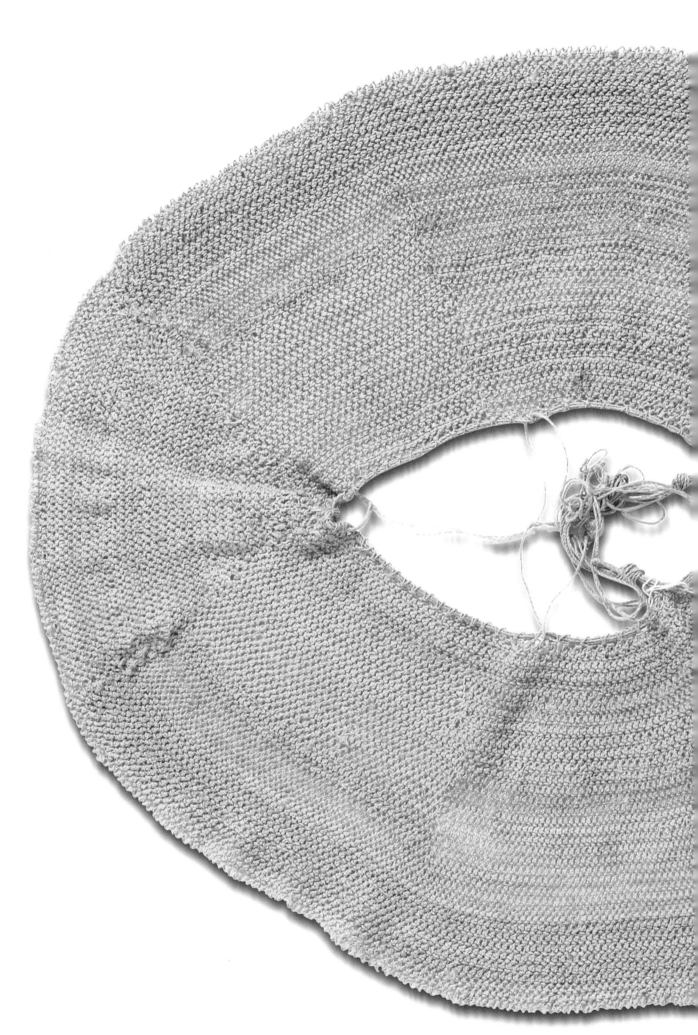

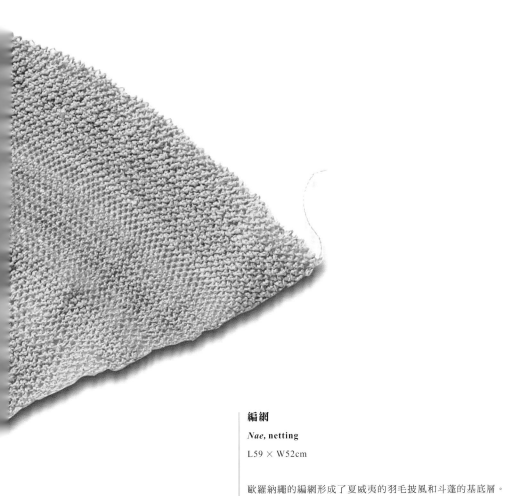

編網

Nae, netting

L59 × W52cm

歐羅納繩的編網形成了夏威夷的羽毛披風和斗蓬的基底層。

Netting of *olonā* cordage forms the foundation for Hawaiian feather capes and cloaks.

手持的「卡希利」

***Kahili pa`a lima*, hand kahili**

H66cm

手持的卡希利是「阿里夷」階級的象徵，他們
出現時就會使用。這件卡希利帕阿里瑪是由染
色的羽毛製成，柄的地方有龜殼和海象牙。

Hand *kahili* were symbolic of the *ali`i* class, and
used in their presence. This *kahili pa`a lima* is
made with dyed feathers and has a handle of turtle
shell and walrus ivory.

「歐羅納」刮具
Olonā scrapers

L23 × W9cm

「歐羅納」刮具
Olonā scrapers

L15 × W6cm

「歐羅納」板
Olonā board

L206 × W9cm

土生的歐羅納（寬葉*Touchardia*）非常受到珍視，它被夏威夷人拿來製作最堅固的繩索。刮下來且經細心處理後的樹皮，在製作漁網、武器和羽毛披風上具有高度的價值。

The native *olonā* (*Touchardia latifolia)* was used for the strongest cordage made by Hawaiians and was greatly treasured. The bark of the plant, scraped and carefully processed, was valued highly in the making of fishing nets, weapons and feather capes.

長牙垂飾項鍊

Lei niho palaoa, necklace with ivory pendant

L27 × W14 × H6cm

早期的夏威夷，只有酋長會戴「類尼侯帕拉歐阿」，長牙垂飾大多建議做成舌頭狀，象徵話語之說與被聽的威信，這是酋長的特權。這個項鍊（或「類」一環）是由人類頭髮的八股細緻髮辮做成的，而頭髮是收集自與戴此項鍊者有親近關係的人。

In ancient Hawai`i, *lei niho palaoa* were only worn by chiefs. It is often suggested that the ivory pendant, shaped like a tongue, represented the authority to speak and be heard a privilege of chiefs. The necklace, or *lei,* was made of human hair arranged in a fine 8-ply braid. The hair was collected from individuals who were closely associated with the person who wore *lei niho palaoa.*

音樂及舞蹈

呼拉舞（hula）的聲音、動作與服飾，激起
了夏威夷群島第一批訪客們的好奇與興趣。
早期的夏威夷，音樂和舞蹈所呈現的不只是
表演而已，透過唱誦、歌曲與舞蹈，夏威夷
人訴說了他們的歷史，榮耀著他們的偉大，
表達他們的情感與想法，並表露他們對神和
各種自然力量的敬意。夏威夷人運用各式各
樣的樂器，來展開一段呼拉舞的節奏，或傳
遞一個特殊訊息。

Music and dance

Hula sounds, motions and costumes intrigued the
first visitors to the Hawaiian Islands. In early
Hawai'i, music and dance represented more than
just a performance. Through chant, song and
dance, Hawaiian shared their history, honored
their great, expressed their emotions and thoughts,
and demonstrated their respect for deities and the
many forces of nature. Hawaiians use a variety
of instruments to set the rhythm for a *hula* or
to convey a special message.

Pele Pukui Suganuma 與 Kaupena Wong 在比夏博物館夏威夷廳的表演

Pele Pukui Suganuma and Kaupena Wong performing in Hawaiian Hall, Bishop Museum, Honolulu, Hawaiʻi.

葫蘆鼓

Ipu heke, gourd drums

H78 × Dia32cm

大大小小的葫蘆鼓是用來為舞者敲打節奏的，這些傳統的樂器在傳統和現代的呼拉舞表演時仍然會使用。

Large and small drums of gourd are used to beat the rhythm for dancers. These traditional implements are still used in performances of traditional and modern hula.

鼓

Pahu, drum

H29 × W17cm

典型的鼓是以椰子樹幹，頂部繃鯊魚皮（或魚）所製成。

Drums were typically made of coconut trunk, with taut shark skin (or fish) stretched over the top.

「庫佩耶」－踝飾

Kupe`e, **ankle rattle**

L40.5 × W27cm

為傳統舞蹈伴奏的聲音，是來自竹子響器、葫蘆鼓、石製響板，以及展示在此的這種腿上的響器。

The sounds that accompanied traditional dance came from bamboo rattles, gourd drums, stone castanets, and leg rattles such as this one.

音樂棒

Kala`au, music sticks

有一些呼拉舞是由特殊的樂器伴奏，這些音樂棒是由舞者使用，敲打出重複的節奏以強調拍子。

Some hula is accompanied by specific musical implements. These music sticks are used by dancers to tap out a repeated pattern to emphasize a beat.

上：L29 × W4cm

下：L40 × W3cm

葫蘆哨

Hōkiokio, gourd whistle

H7 × Cir17.5cm

簡單的樂器其吹奏需要技術，它為傳統音樂的聲音增加了多樣性。有一些樂器，例如侯其歐其歐，
也可以用來傳送愛人間的訊息，而那讓熱心的傳教士感到不滿。

Simple instrument were played with skill, adding a variety of tones to traditional music. Some implements,

such as the *hōkiokio*, could also be used to impart messages between lovers, and were frowned upon by zealous missionaries.

在庫克船長面前舉行的拳擊競賽
Boxing match before Capt. Cook

消遣

運動競技

一整年的曆程中會有一段期間，一切的戰事皆休止，用來付稅並舉行運動
競技。這段「瑪卡希基」的季節大約從11月開始直到2月底，最佳的競技者
會參與各項競賽，展現力量與技藝。

Recreation

Sports competition

The annual calendar included a period when all warfare was halted, taxes were paid
and sports competition took place. This Makahiki season extended from the about
November through February. The best competitors engaged in various matches,
showing their strength and skills.

石製遊戲圓盤

`Ulu maika, stone game disks

H5 × Dia7.5cm

石製遊戲圓盤

`Ulu maika, stone game disks

H2.5 × Dia5cm

石製遊戲圓盤

`Ulu maika, stone game disks

H6.5 × Dia14cm

夏威夷人利用滾石盤來競賽，若非讓石盤滾動一段長距離，就是從一段距離外精確地將它滾過兩木樁之間。選對具有適當尺寸與重量的石盤，有助於熟練的玩手獲得成功。小一點的圓盤能夠滾長一點的距離，但是當地表面條件有所改變時，它就會離開原來的筆直路線。

Hawaiians competed by bowling these stone disks over long distances, or by rolling them precisely between two pegs a good distance away. Choosing the right disks of appropriate size and weight contributed to the success of a skilled player. Smaller disks could travel a longer distance but would be set off a straight path when they encountered changes in the surface of the ground.

滑標

Moa pahe`e, sliding darts

L37 × Dia5cm

L38.5 × Dia4cm

這些單邊尖細狀的木標被用在一種滑動的遊戲中，目標點設在一段距離外，以此遊戲來賭博是很平常的。

These tapered wooden darts were used in a sliding game where distance was the goal, and betting was common.

標

Pahe`e, dart

L72 × Dia2cm

這件鏢最初可能是斷掉的魚叉尖端,稍後才被用來製作遊戲的用具。

It is probable that this dart originally is the tip of a broken spear, latter used as a game piece.

在大島 Kealakekua 灣拋網叉魚的漁夫
Hawaiian throw net and spear fishermen, Kealakekua Bay, Hawai'i.

衝浪板

Papa he'e nalu, surfboard

L131 × W28 × T2cm

伍茲收藏，受贈於1935年

Woods Collection, received in 1935

衝浪板的夏威夷語字面上的意思是「滑浪的板子」，衝浪是酋長的運動，男女都一樣，傳說流傳：在威基基海岸外曾出現過酋長們的衝浪競賽。衝浪板的尺寸大小，從約略15英尺長150磅重的，到在此展示的這件這麼小的。大型的衝浪板需要技巧、平衡感和力量才能成功地騎乘一段長距離。

The Hawaiian term for surfboards is literally "board for sliding waves." Surfing was the sport of chiefs, both male and female. Legends tell of competition between chiefs that occurred outside the shore at Waīkīkī. Surfboards ranged in size from approximately 15 feet in length and 150 pounds in weight to small ones such as this one. The larger boards required skill, balance and strength for a successful long ride.

檀香山威基基，夏威夷男子與衝浪板
Native Hawaiian man with surfboard, Waikiki, Honolulu, Hawaiʻi

獨木舟（模型）

Wa`a, **canoe (model)**

L60 × W30 × H12cm

獨木舟的需求衰減後，製舟者轉而製作獨木舟模型。在十九世紀的轉變時期，蒐藏獨木舟模型變得盛行。

這件模型所描繪出的此型獨木舟，過去曾用於靠近海岸線的地方，做短距離航行、釣魚或消遣用。

As the need for functional canoes waned, canoe makers turned to making models. During the turn of the 19th century, collecting such canoe models became popular.

The type of canoe depicted by this model is one used near the coastline for short distance travel, fishing or recreation.

獨木舟（模型）

Wa`a, **canoe (model)**

L30 × W20 × H72cm

現代的模型製造者富士摩托示範了這種用來做長距離航行的雙舟獨木舟。

A modern model maker, Fujimoto demonstrated the kind of double-hull canoe that was used for longer voyages.

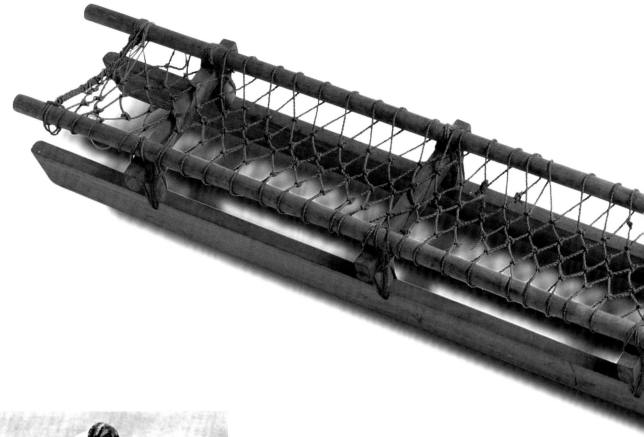

侯路阿騎乘示範
Hōlua riding demonstration

長橇

Papa hōlua, sled

L177 × W26 × H16cm

細長形的長橇最長到12英尺,是愛冒險的夏威夷運動家在玩的,草坡滑道由上往下可能延伸幾哩長,長橇可以由一人搭乘,一旦乘行開始有一點控制住後,就可以施力了,據說這些運動家可以達到一個小時40英哩的速度。

侯路阿的乘行現在又再度恢復,然而,只有最大膽的運動員會接受這個挑戰。

Slender sleds, often up to 12 feet long were ridden by adventurous Hawaiian athletes. The course down grassy slopes and could extend for miles. The sled could accommodate one rider, and once the ride began little control could be exerted. It is said that these athletes could reach speeds of 40 miles an hour.

Hōlua riding is now experiencing a comeback, though only the hardiest of sportsmen will take the challenge.

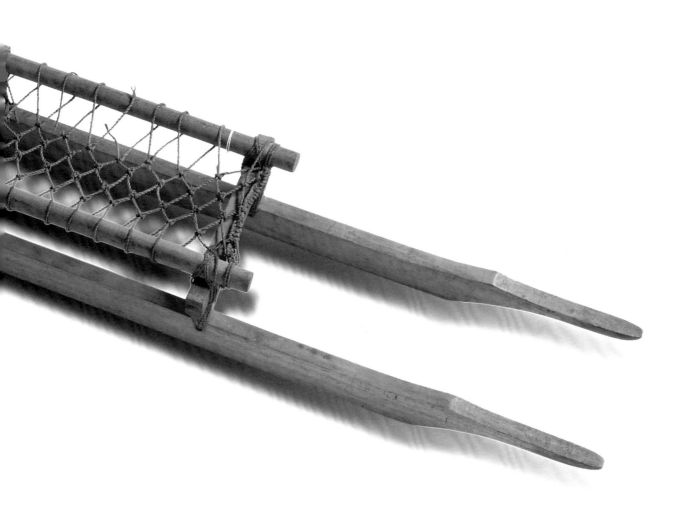

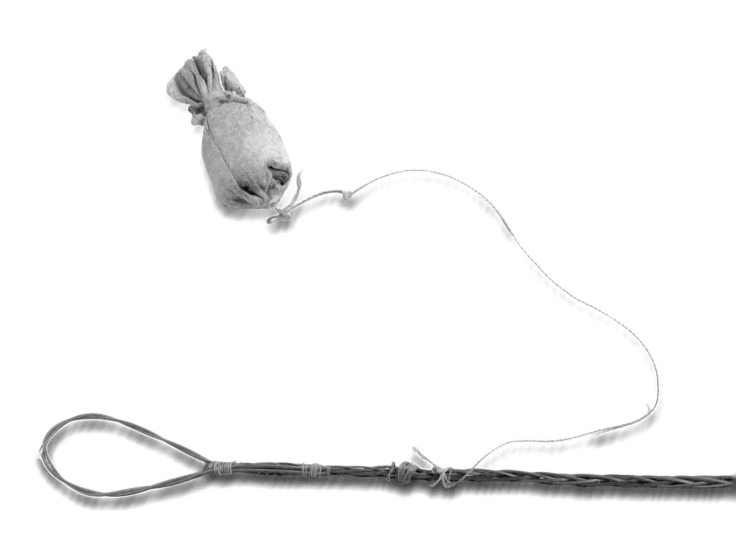

球與環的遊戲

Pala`ie, ball and loop game

L74cm　ball 5cm

這是夏威夷版的球與杯遊戲。椰葉中脈編的辮子一端有一個環，一顆樹皮布球繫在繩子上，並連接於環的下方，遊戲的目的是要有節奏地擺盪以讓球進入環中。通常這個遊戲附帶著唱頌。

The Hawaiian version of the cup-and-ball game included of braid of coconut midribs with a loop at one end and a tapa ball on a string attached below the loop. The object of the game was to rhythmically swing and catch the ball in the loop. The game was often accompanied by a chant.

外來者的到來
Arrival of Foreigners

外來者抵達夏威夷

西元1778年1月18日，詹姆士·庫克船長（James Cook）以及決心號（Resolution）和發現號（Discovery）船隊上的人們，首度瞥見航海圖尚未記載的夏威夷群島。最先進入眼簾的是歐胡島和考艾島，然後是尼豪島。兩天後，這些英國人在考艾島的威美亞（Waimea）落下船錨。

庫克對夏威夷人的印象深刻，他們的生活型態與性情令人感到愉悅並有條理。他和同行者與夏威夷人從事交易，自由交換鐵製品、珠鍊與鏡子等，用以補給他們的必需品。他記錄了酋長們所穿戴的做工精細的羽毛斗蓬，以及其他出色的工藝品。

後來，發生了小艇被偷的爭端，庫克也因而死於夏威夷島，時值西元1779年1月16日。

Foreigners come to Hawai`i

On January 18, 1778, Captain James Cook and those on board his ships, the *Resolution* and the *Discovery*, caught the first glimpse of the uncharted Hawaiian Island chain. The islands of O`ahu, Kaua`i, and then Ni`ihau were sighted, and two days later, the Englishmen set anchor at Waimea, Kaua`i.

Cook was impressed with the Hawaiian people, whose lifestyles and dispositions were pleasant and orderly. He and his men engaged in trade with Hawaiians, freely exchanging iron objects, beads and mirrors to replenish his provisions. He took note of the finel y made feather cloaks worn by the chiefs, and other items of excellent craftsmanship.

One January 16, 1779, Cook perished on the island of Hawai`i after an altercation over a stolen cutter.

1778年外科醫師威廉·艾利斯和庫克船長一起航行，他是首位見到夏威夷群島鍊的人，這件細緻的藝術品描繪了當船靠近這些島嶼海岸線時的景色。

Surgeon William Ellis sailed with Captain Cook who first encountered the chain of Hawaiian Islands in 1778. This delicate works of art depict view from the ships as they approached the coastlines of the islands.

1778年，夏威夷之阿托瓦島景觀，阿托威與國王山

Views of Atowa, one of the Hawaiian, Atowi and the King's Mount, 1778

Part of the West-Side of Owhaow, one of the Sandwich Islands.

Owhyhee.

1779年，在夏威夷對庫克的進貢
An offering before Captain Cook in the Hawaiian, 1779

早期夏威夷的生活

夏威夷人通力合作，將自然的資源做最佳的運用， 他們深深地尊敬大自然，以及這片支持他們生存的土地。

「阿胡璞哇亞」（*Ahupua`a*）是傳統的土地分區方式，包含從山岳（*mauka*，毛卡）到海洋（*makai*，馬凱）的不同生態區，每個「阿胡璞哇亞」都涵括了生存所需的各種資源。淡水受到悉心的管理，以供應飲水、盥洗與灌溉所需；野生與人工培育的各種動植物 ，提供了食物、衣著、工具及其他所需物質。因此，大自然提供的這些禮物，收穫的時節需要長者的智慧加以引導。

夏威夷人享受舞蹈和音樂，男女皆參與這些活動。在禮讚神祇、慶祝大自然或榮耀過去和現在的英雄時，經常會表演「美樂」（*mele*，詩歌形式的口傳傳統歌曲）。

庫克船長的船隊藝術家約翰‧偉伯（John Webber），對夏威夷型式的衣著與裝飾非常感興趣，因此，細心記錄了他所見到的各種活動，這些詳盡的圖畫後來被出版。

Life in early Hawai‘i

Hawaiians worked together to make the best use of available natural resources, and deeply respected nature and the land that supported their existence.

Ahupua`a,* were traditional land divisions that included different ecological zones from mountain *(mauka)* to ocean *(makai)*. Each *ahupua`a contained all the resources required for survival. Fresh water was managed carefully for drinking, bathing and irrigation. Wild and cultivated plants and animals provided food, clothing, tools and other needed materials. The harvesting of nature's gifts was guided by the wisdom of the elders.

Hawaiians enjoyed dance and music, and both men and women participated. *Mele*, songs, were often performed in praise of the gods, to celebrate nature or to honor heroes of the past and present.

Captain Cook's ship artist, John Webber, was intrigued with the Hawaiian style of clothing and ornamentation. He carefully documented the activities of the Hawaiian people he encountered. His impressions were recorded with detailed illustrations that were later published.

羽毛飾品區別出阿里夷或酋長階級的成員，羽環－雷呼魯瑪奴（*lei hulu manu*）－是戴在頭頂或肩上，羽環後來的變化型是羽毛帽帶，它在西式的帽子流行時變得廣為風行。

夏威夷的女孩

A girl of the Hawaiian

Feather adornments distinguished members of the *ali'i* or chiefly class. Feather lei, *lei hulu manu*, were worn on the crown of the head, or on the shoulders. A later version of the feather lei is the feather hatband, made popular as western style hats became fashionable.

羽環

Lei hulu manu, feather lei

L64 × W4cm

這件精美的羽環是由目前已經絕種的「歐歐」鳥
（ʻōʻō，*Acrulocercus nobilis*）的明亮羽毛所製。
歐歐鳥是一種身上只有少數黃色羽毛的黑鳥。

This exquisite lei is made from the bright feathers of the ʻōʻō bird
(*Acrulocercus nobilis*), now extinct. The ʻōʻō is primarily a black
bird with just a few yellow feathers.

歐歐鳥 ʻŌʻŌ *Acrulocercus nobilis*

偉伯細心的素描夏威夷原住民的刺青圖樣，典型的刺青用梳子和針是由鳥骨所製成的，然而，只有少數早期的物品仍然存在著。刺青現在在夏威夷再度風行，儘管使用的是現代的方法和器具，今日所見的許多圖樣是立基於18世紀和19世紀初的早期航行藝術所記錄的。

Webber carefully sketched the tattoo patterns of the native Hawaiians. Tattooing combs and needles were typically made from bird bone, though few early examples still exist. Tattooing in Hawai'i is enjoying renewed popularity. Though modern techniques and implements are now used, many of the patterns seen today are based on those captured in early voyaging art of the 18th and early 19th centuries.

夏威夷半邊臉刺青的男人

Man of the Hawaiian, half face tattooed

刺青梳子

Tattooing comb

L28.6 × W6.2cm stiker L41.5 × W1.5cm

科歐納・孚納斯 製作及出借

Made and loaned by Keone Nunes

孚納斯是一位文化工作者，在夏威夷刺青的藝術與技法上表現突出，儘管此刺青梳是由現代材質所製造，但是，它是從早期的物品複製而來的。

Keone Nuncs is a recognized cultural practitioner who excels in the art and protocol of Hawaiian tattooing. His tattooing comb replicates early ones though it is made of modern materials.

在此所見的是一名男子的四種舞姿，這位舞者所用的樂器包括「巫里巫里」（'uli 'uli，葫蘆鈴鼓）
和穿在腳上的「庫佩耶」（küpe'e）。

夏威夷跳舞的男子，1780年

Man of the Hawaiian, dancing, ca. 1780

Four poses of a male dancer are shown here. The instruments used by this dancer include 'uli 'uli (gourd rattles)
and küpe'e (worn on the legs).

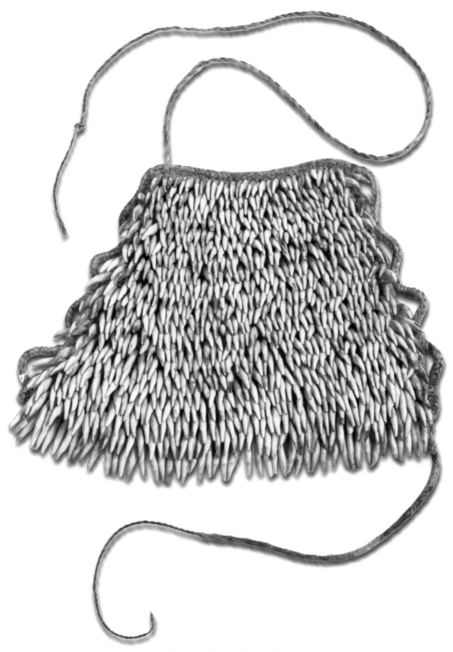

庫佩耶，狗牙嘎嘎器

Küpe`e, **dog teeth rattle**

L36 × W27cm

由許多隻狗的牙齒所製，並且以最堅固的繩子綁在一起，當舞者的移動具有韻律與強度時，嘎嘎器會發出悅耳的聲音。

Made from the canine teeth of many dogs, and bound together with the strongest cordage, these rattles made a pleasing sound as the dancer moved with rhythm and strength.

乘坐獨木舟的人看起來是在運送被包裹著具有宗教意義的雕像,他們戴著裝飾了條狀樹皮布和葉子的葫蘆頭盔,這些葫蘆頭盔通常被認定為戰士的頭盔,因此它們極有可能表示戴頭盔者與宗教活動執行者的階級有關。

The passengers on the canoe appear to be transporting wrapped images of religious significance. They wear gourd helmets decorated with strips of *kapa* and foliage. While these gourds are often identified as warrior helmets, it is more probable that they signaled that the wearer was associated with a class of religious practitioners.

夏威夷的獨木舟,戴防護面具的槳手們
A canoe of the Hawaiian, the rowers masked

以約翰・偉伯的藝術作品為基礎的刻畫
Engraving based on art by John Webber

葫蘆頭盔

Gourd helmet

H58 × Cir100cm

現代複製品

Modern replica

早期葫蘆頭盔的完整樣品並不存在，偉伯等藝術家的插圖提供了它們曾經存在的證據以及它們可能的重要性。

Complete examples of early gourd helmets do not exist. The illustrations of artists such as John Webber provide evidence of their existence and their probable significance.

島嶼的轉變
Change in the Islands

卡美哈美哈大帝
Kamehameha the Great

統一的王國新政府

卡美哈美哈大帝（Kamehameha the Great）與庫克船長相遇時才二十出頭，在那次會面之後，幾年內卡美哈美哈便展現了他的軍事本領，掌控整個夏威夷島。到了1810年，他藉由軍事力量與和平談判，成功統一了整個夏威夷群島。

西元1780年代之前，外國船隻來訪的比率增加。卡美哈美哈了解到西方人的造訪已是必然，因此，他巧妙地將夏威夷傳統與外來者所引進的有利作法相互結合，舊有的酋長制度遭到了廢除，群島各地酋長們的權力也被縮小。他慎選諫臣，並將忠心的非夏威夷人士納入顧問團。卡美哈美哈的力量與智慧，讓夏威夷迎接了一段和平興盛的時期。

A united kingdom, a new government.

Kamehameha the Great was in his early twenties when he met Captain Cook. Within a few years of that meeting, Kamehameha demonstrated his military prowess and established control over the island of Hawai`i. By 1810, he successfully unified the island chain by military might as well as by peaceful negotiation.

By the 1780s, foreign ships arrived with increasing frequency. Recognizing that the Westerners were not to be turned away, Kamehameha skillfully married the best of Hawaiian traditions with the beneficial ways introduced by foreigners. The old system of chiefdoms was abolished, and the power of chiefs throughout the Islands diminished. He chose his advisers carefully, and included loyal non-Hawaiians among his counsel. Kamehameha's might and wisdom ushered in a period of peace and prosperity for Hawai'i.

外來影響力的增加

卡美哈美哈對外國人的接受，為貿易成長鋪好一條路。毛皮貿易考察隊行旅於北太平洋時，為了補給必需品，造訪了夏威夷的幾個港口。獲利豐富的檀香生意因而開始，並讓夏威夷與中國有了往來。然而，除了開創新的稅收來源與貿易機會外，外國人也帶來了新的宗教信仰及生活型態，這使得夏威夷傳統的力量受到侵蝕。

西元1819年是關鍵性的一年。卡美哈美哈大帝在5月去世，紐約的公理會傳教士搭船前往夏威夷群島，同年的11月，卡美哈美哈二世的一些舉動，瓦解了傳統的「卡曝」（*kapu*，禁忌）體系。這三個事件激起了往後幾年發生的戲劇化轉變。

Foreign influence grows

Kamehameha's acceptance of foreigners paved the way to increased trade. Fur trading expeditions visited Hawaiian ports for provisioning during trips in the northern Pacific. A profitable sandalwood business developed and linked Hawai`i to China. However, besides creating new sources of revenue and trade opportunities, foreigners brought new religious beliefs and lifestyles that eroded the strength of Hawaiian traditions.

1819 was a pivotal year. Kamehameha the Great died in May. Congregationalist missionaries from New York embarked on their way to the Hawaiian Islands. The traditional *kapu* (taboo) system was dissolved by actions of Kamehameha II in November of the same year. These three events stimulated the dramatic change that took place in succeeding years.

臂膀用針釦

Coat of arms brooch

Dia4.6cm

夏威夷人的手臂針釦源自於卡美哈美哈三世統治期間(1825-1854)，他的私人秘書提摩太歐·哈利力歐乘船到美國、法國和大不列顛，去確保他們對於夏威夷獨立的同意，此外，也取到夏威夷政府的紋飾。這個紋飾是1843年購於倫敦的，座右銘「*Ua mau ke ea o ka aina I ka pono*」出現在紋飾上的意思是「這片土地的生命因公義而永垂不朽」。它是從卡美哈美哈三世的演講中節錄下來的，當時的夏威夷群島經過英國爵士袍雷六個月的統治後，其主權由不列顛政府歸還給夏威夷的酋長。

這個別針開始時極可能是作為大釦子來使用，用以將厚重的衣物固定在肩上。在別針的背面有一個用中文字寫的製造商標誌，推測它可能是經由一位移民至夏威夷群島的中國珠寶商人所製。

The Hawaiian Coat of Arms originated during the rule of Kamehameha III (1825 1854). His personal secretary, Timoteo Haalilio, sailed to the U.S., France, and Great Britain to secure agreements to guarantee Hawaiian independence, and additionally, to obtain a Hawaiian crest of government. The crest was purchased in London in 1843. The motto, "*Ua mau ke ea o ka aina I ka pono*" that appears on the crest means "The life of the land is perpetuated by righteousness. It was taken from speech given by Kamehameha III after the British government returned the sovereignty of the Islands to Hawaiian *ali'i* after a six month period when rule was controlled by the English Lord Paulet.

This pin most likely originated as a large button used to fasten a heavy garment around one's shoulders. The back shows a maker's mark using a Chinese character, suggesting that it was made by a Chinese jeweler who migrated to the Hawaiian Islands.

夏威夷的製幣也是在卡美哈美哈三世統治的期間被引進，並且在卡拉卡瓦治理的期間(1874-1891)重新建立，在夏威夷的君主統治被推翻之後，夏威夷的製幣並沒有再繼續，而所遺留下來的錢幣通常會被製作成可供蒐藏的首飾，例如這件卡拉卡瓦一角硬幣製成的腰帶。

Hawaiian coinage was also introduce during the reign of Kamehameha III, and re-established during the rule of Kalākaua (1874-1891). After the over throw of the Hawaiian monarchy, Hawaiian coinage was discontinued and remaining pieces were often made into collectible jewelry, such as this belt of Kalākaua dimes.

夏威夷錢幣製成的腰帶
Belt of Hawaiian coins
L77 × W3.7cm

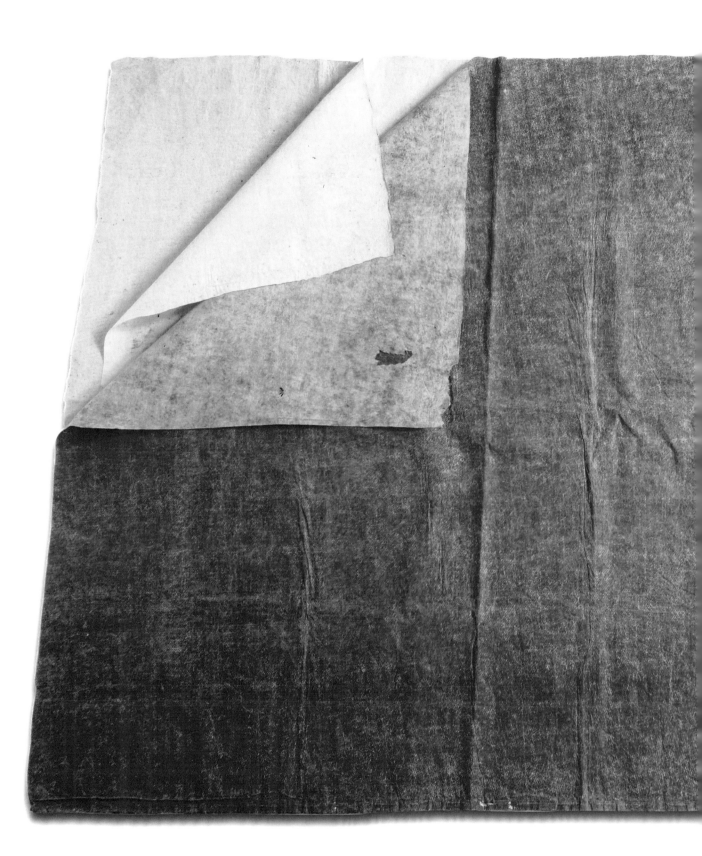

「卡帕摩耶」－睡覺用的樹皮布

Kapa moe, sleeping kapa

L245 × W165cm

即便是傳統的樹皮布也受到外國人引進的東西
的影響，此卡帕摩耶的顏色在紅色衣物進入後
變得流行，為了要創造出玫瑰粉色，線狀纖維
從紅色布料中取出，並且被敲打進樹皮布中，
唯有在放大鏡的檢視下，才能夠看出這個為樹
皮布染色的新方法。

Even tradition barkcloth was affected by the
introductions brought by foreigners. The color of
kapa moe became popular after the arrival of red
cloth. In order to create the rosy pink color,
thread fibers were remove from red fabric and
beaten into the barkcloth. Only upon inspection
with a magnifying glass will one see this new
method of coloring *kapa*!

夏威夷襯墊絎縫枕頭

Hawaiian quilt pillow

L58.5 × W57cm

黛柏拉‧卡卡利亞製作
Made by Deborah "Kepola" Umiamaka Kakalia

2005年收藏自萩依女士
From Mrs. Herbert Y.C. Choy in 2005

這個枕頭的製作者曾說過，在她一生中，至少做了75個大型棉被，
和3,000個襯墊絎縫的枕頭。

The maker of this pillow once stated that she had made at least 75 large
bed quilts and 3,000 quilted pillows during her lifetime.

夏威夷製被的指導者 Debbie Kepola Kakalia在比夏博物館的Atherton Halau製被
Debbie Kepola Kakalia, Hawaiian quilting instructor quilting at Atherton Hālau, Bishop Museum, Honolulu, Hawaiï.

據說在夏威夷的君主政權被推翻後，被稱為「庫烏哈耶夏威夷」（鍾愛的夏威夷旗幟）
的夏威夷旗被就被私下地製作與陳列。

It is said that after the overthrow of the Hawaiian monarchy, Hawaiian flag quilts, called *Kuu Hae Hawaii*
(Beloved Flag of Hawai'i), were made and displayed privately.

夏威夷旗被
Hawaiian flag quilt

L224.2 × W208.3cm

在檀香山威基基Ala Moana公園製作夏威夷被的女人們
Women making Hawaiian quilt at Ala Moana Park, Waikīkī, Honolulu, Hawaïi.

棉被

***Pīkake* and Tuberose Quilt**

L218.4 × W218.4cm

漢娜‧卡敏斯‧貝克製作
Made by Hannah Cummings Baker

棉被製作的技術是傳教士教授酋長階級的年輕女性的，縫紉與製被
被認為是有教養女性的技術，且是針對年輕酋長的訓練，以便讓他
們準備好去面對西方世界。

拼布棉被是夏威夷女性們在首度的縫紉課程中完成的，很快地，製
被者仰賴著他們敏銳的觀察力，以及對夏威夷人來說的天生創造精
神，發展出一種新的棉被，新圖樣通常是植物和花卉的剪影圖，小
心地剪裁，然後嵌飾於一塊單純的布料上，夏威夷棉被包含了「回
聲」製作，即重複嵌飾圖樣，隨旁著用小針縫法縫製出相同圖樣。

Quilt making was a skill that missionaries taught to the young women of
chiefly rank. Sewing and quilt making were considered skills for cultured
women and the training for young *ali'i* to prepare them for encounters
with the Western world.

Patchwork quilts were among the first sewing projects completed by
Hawaiian women. Soon, however, the quilt makers relied on their keen
observation and the creative spirits natural to Hawaiians to develop a new
kind of quilt. The new patterns often were the shadow images of plants
and flowers, carefully cut , then appliquéd to a solid field of fabric.
Hawaiian quilts include "echo" quilting, tiny stitches that follow and
repeat the pattern of the appliqué.

Chun Poon (第一排右側)一家人
Chun Poon family (lt.-rt.)

農場衣物
Plantation clothing

製糖與鳳梨農場內的工作是辛苦的，女性工作者尤其會好好保護他們的皮膚，以免讓太陽曬傷或植物割傷。日本女性穿著的衣物通常能夠指出他們位於日本的故鄉所在區。

十九世紀晚期到二十世紀初移民夏威夷的那些人，他們所穿戴的衣物的樣式與顏色，對於夏威夷的流行時尚有著極大的影響。

Work in the sugar and pineapple plantations was difficult. Female workers especially took care to protect their skin from the sun and from plants that would scratch and cut. Patterns of fabric worn by Japanese women workers often indicated their home prefecture in Japan.

Clothing styles and colors worn by those migrating to Hawai'i during the late 19th century and into the 20th century had a great impact on popular Hawaiian trends.

大眾化的夏威夷
Popular Hawai`i

這些顯眼的插畫曾經是成功的促銷作品，它們將夏威夷群島描繪成一個具有異國風味又浪漫的訪客目的地。

Bold illustrations depicting the Islands as an exotic and romantic destination for the visitor were successful promotional pieces.

菜單封面
Menu covers

將夏威夷行銷到全世界

夏威夷在19世紀的最重要產業是觀光，它在1800年代末便已奠下根基。外國企業發現這個群島提供了極佳的投資機會，他們與夏威夷政府間的協議，以及夏威夷與美國於1876年簽訂的重要互惠條約，帶來了經濟繁榮、新的貿易協定，以及湧入當地的企業家、新居民和醒目的觀光客。

1893年夏威夷君主政體被推翻，緊接著在1898年，整個群島被美國併吞。政治統治者的轉換，也支持了投資與產業成長的持續。那些掌權者認識到商業利益來自於「造訪者、觀光客與健康休閒的追求者」，因此，著手將這個群島塑造成一個具吸引力且浪漫的觀光客天堂。

夏威夷的觀光業，在1930年代之前便席捲了整個群島。豪華飯店、明亮的阿羅哈服裝、迷人的紀念品，以及威基基（Waikīkī）的海灘男孩所彈奏的悅耳、朗朗上口的「烏庫勒樂」（`ukulele，四弦琴）音樂－這些東西將夏威夷「推銷」給許多來此尋求浪漫的島嶼探索之旅的觀光客。

Selling Hawai`i to the world.

Hawai`i's most important industry of the 19[th] century, tourism, had roots in the late 1800s. Foreign businesses had found that the Islands provided good investment opportunities. Favorable agreements with the Hawaiian government, and the significant reciprocity treaty of 1876 between Hawai`i and the United States resulted in an economic boom, new trade treaties, and an influx of entrepreneurs, new residents and prominent visitors.

The overthrow of the Hawaiian Monarchy in 1893 was followed by the annexation of Islands in 1898. This shift in political control supported continued investment and growth of industry. Those in power recognized the commercial benefit to be derived from "visitors, sightseers, and health-and-recreation seekers," and set about to make the Islands an attractive and romantic visitor haven.

By the 1930s, tourism had engulfed the Hawaiian Islands. Luxury hotels, bright "aloha" clothing, charming souvenirs, and catchy `ukulele music played by beach boys on Waikīkī Beach these things "sold" Hawai`i to the many tourists who sought a romantic island adventure.

檀香山威基基夏威夷皇家飯店的兩位呼拉舞者Lily Padeken Wai (右) 和 Leolani Blaisdell (左)

Hula dancers Lily Padeken Wai (right) and Leolani Blaisdell (left), at the Royal Hawaiian Hotel, Waikīkī, Honolulu, Hawaiʻi.

姆姆

Holokū style *muʻumuʻu*

H231 × L672cm (含摺邊)

姆姆

Holokū style *muʻumuʻu*

H200 × L750cm (含摺邊)

侯櫻庫長袍在1940年代之前流行起來，目前仍舊是婚禮等慶典的特色。

Holokū gowns became popular by the 1940s, and are still featured in celebrations such as weddings.

Kalakaua國王的宮廷呼拉舞者

Hawaiian hula dancers from King Kalakaua's court, Hawai'i; Pauahi in center

四弦琴

`*Ukulele*

L59 × W19cm

李奧納多‧孥納斯製造
Made by Leonardo Nunes

這件四弦琴在1916年取得版權，是夏威夷最早期三位四弦琴製造者之一的後裔所製，四弦琴是以1879年被帶到這群島的葡萄牙樂器「布雷金哈」（*braginha*）為基礎所製造的。尤克萊利的字面意思是「跳躍的跳蚤」，所以我們可以想像隨著音樂背創造出來時，樂師的手指在琴桁間飛舞。

This `ukulele, copyrighted in 1916, was made by a descendant of one of the three earliest `ukulele makers in Hawai'i. The `ukulele was based on a Portuguese instrument called the *braginha* brought to the Islands in 1879. `Ukulele literally means "leaping flea" and one can imaging the musician's fingers hopping from fret to fret as music was created.

手拿四弦琴的夏威夷女子
Hawaiian woman with ʻukulele, Hawaiʻi.
青版照相法。
Cyanotype

穿戴花環的夏威夷女子
Hawaiian woman wearing lei, Hawai'i.

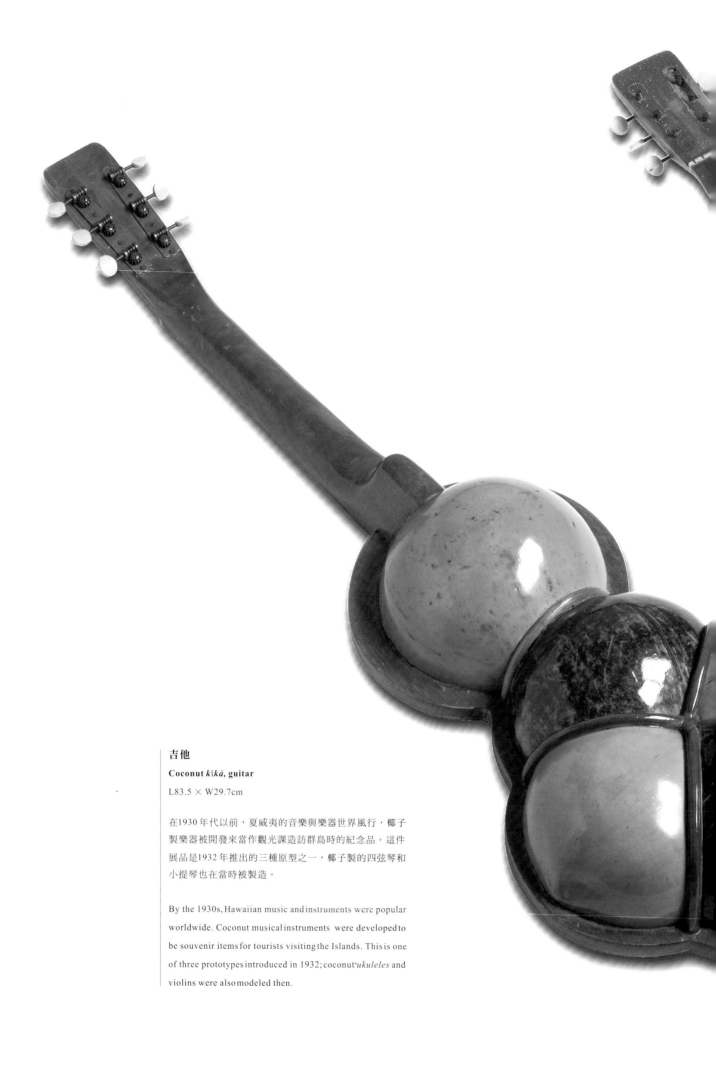

吉他

Coconut *kīkā*, guitar

L83.5 × W29.7cm

在1930年代以前，夏威夷的音樂與樂器世界風行，椰子
製樂器被開發來當作觀光課造訪群島時的紀念品。這件
展品是1932年推出的三種原型之一，椰子製的四弦琴和
小提琴也在當時被製造。

By the 1930s, Hawaiian music and instruments were popular
worldwide. Coconut musical instruments were developed to
be souvenir items for tourists visiting the Islands. This is one
of three prototypes introduced in 1932; coconut *ukuleles* and
violins were also modeled then.

查理斯・理德・比夏和伯妮絲・帕娃希・比夏
Charles Reed and Bernice Pauahi Bishop.

比夏博物館
Bishop Museum

伯妮絲・帕娃希・比夏博物館

卡美哈美哈大帝最後一代的直系血親伯妮絲・帕娃亥・比夏（Bernice Pauahi Bishop）公主死於1884年，1889年，她的丈夫查理・理德・比夏（Charles Reed Bishop）創立比夏博物館，以榮耀他的亡妻。她個人與另外兩位重要女人露絲・凱葉理寇拉妮公主（Ruth Ke`elikōlani）和愛瑪拉妮王后（Queen Emalani）所擁有的物品，構成了這個新博物館的基礎典藏品。在查理・理德・比夏的帶領下，博物館變成了「一個永續存在的教育來源，不僅針對夏威夷人，也針對其他對玻里尼西亞民族學與自然歷史感興趣之人」。

今日，比夏博物館在文化與自然史蒐藏方面舉世聞名，對於夏威夷與太平洋地區的自然及文化環境的再發現、保存及鑑賞也做出了貢獻。目前的典藏品包括：超過120萬件的文化物品，以及2200萬件的科學收藏標本。透過在它各個場地的不同活動，以及許多教育推廣活動，博物館每年都服務著無數的參觀者與研究人員。

比夏博物館座落在歐胡島檀香山（Honolulu）的市郊。

Bernice Pauahi Bishop Museum

Princess Bernice Pauahi Bishop, the last direct descendant of Kamehameha the Great, died in 1884. In 1889, her husband, Charles Reed Bishop, founded Bishop Museum to honor his late wife. Her personal possessions and those of two other chiefly women, Princess Ruth Ke`elikōlani and Queen Emalani formed the founding collections of the new museum. Under C.R. Bishop's guidance, the Bishop Museum became an institution to serve as "a permanent source of instruction, not only to this people, but to all others interested in Polynesian Ethnology and Natural History."

Today, Bishop Museum's cultural and natural history collections are world renown, and contribute to the rediscovery, preservation, and appreciation of the natural and cultural environments of Hawai'i and the Pacific. Its collections are made up of over 1.2 million cultural objects and over 22 million specimens in the science collections. The Museum serves thousands of visitors and researchers annually, through programs on its various sites, as well as through a multitude of educational outreach programs.

Bishop Museum is located on the outskirts of Honolulu on the island of O`ahu.

夏威夷檀香山比夏博物館
Bishop Museum, Honolulu, Hawai'i

重新取得傳統知識
Reclaiming traditional knowledge

二十世紀前半段，本土語言與傳統的運用急遽減少，直到六〇年代，有一個冒險家世代開始想要恢復處於失傳危機的傳統知識。

這些冒險家以一些大學為根據地，那是復甦夏威夷語以及夏威夷文化的核心所在。夏威夷語發生了一場重生，儘管是透過教科書在課堂中傳授，而非經由家庭成員在家裡教導。夏威夷語的再興鋪陳了一條道路，讓人得以努力取得其他傳統的夏威夷智慧與才能，而一些帶有此類目標的主要計畫也紛紛成立。

傳統的玻里尼西亞航海方式是夏威夷文化的起源，因此，它變成恢復文化知識的主要努力所在。航海獨木舟「侯庫類阿號」（Hokulea）的建造，以及它在1975年的首航，確認了一條令人興奮的路，讓人得以了解早期夏威夷人的工作與技藝，年輕的航海員和船員首度體驗不使用現代儀器而航行於太平洋。

1980年代末期，新的冒險家想要重建傳統獨木舟，同時努力重新掌握多種的傳統技藝，讓它們回歸到日常生活實踐中。除了製作獨木舟的技藝之外，他們也探究了傳統船帆的編織、栽種製作繩索用的夏威夷植物、綑綁的技術，以及傳統禮節的合宜表達方式。儘管有許多重要的挑戰及嘗試，「夏威夷洛亞號」（Hawai`iloa）以第一個發現夏威夷群島的人而命名，它的成功，被認為是重新恢復夏威夷認同及傳統的主要一步。

夏威夷洛亞號細部
Detail of *Hawai‘iloa*

接近完成階段的夏威夷洛亞號
Hawai‘iloa in its completing phase of construction

Practice of native language and tradition decreased dramatically in the first half of the 20th century . By the 1960s , a generation of adventurers set about to reclaim traditional knowledge that was at risk of being lost.

Such adventurers were found at the universities, the heart of the renewed interest in Hawaiian language and culture. A rebirth of Hawaiian language took place, though now was taught with textbooks and in classrooms rather than by family members at home. The resurgence of the Hawaiian language gave way to efforts to claim other traditional Hawaiian wisdom and talents, and major programs with those goals were instituted.

Traditional Polynesian voyaging, the very origin of the Hawaiian culture, became the core of efforts to reclaim cultural knowledge. The construction of the voyaging canoe Hokulea, and its first launching in 197 5, identified an exciting path to understanding early Hawaiian practices and skills. Young navigators and seaman had their first experiences in traveling the Pacific without the use of modern instruments.

By the late 1980s, new adventurers sought to reconstruct traditional canoes in an effort to recapture many traditional skills and place these back into practice. Beside the art of canoe making, the weaving of traditional sails, the cultivation of Hawaiian plants to make cordage, techniques in lashing, and the appropriate expressions of cultural protocol were explored. Though there were significant challenges and trials, the success of the Hawai`iloa, named for the first discoverer of the Hawaiian Islands, is considered a major step in reclaiming Hawaiian identity and traditions.

夏威夷的當代藝術

1975年，詹森（Rocky Kaiouliokahihikoloehu Jensen）成立了一個年輕夏威夷藝術家的協會，他們在藝術創作上強調「夏威夷性」（Hawaiianess）。為了要實現這點，成員們被鼓勵去研究各種類型的傳統知識，他們所創造的當代藝術，是對於古老知識的一項表達，如同詹森所說的：

> 『文化是一種活生生的實體，應當隨著時代成長與改變。因此，若要了解我們的今日，必得先認識並了解我們的過去，因為今日各項問題的解決之道就存在那裡。現今文化所採取的型態必定在過去就立下根基…，唯有如此我們才能為現代文化賦予新的意義，並確保我們未來的安全。』

詹森在這裡展示的藝術作品，是由打造夏威夷洛亞號所遺留的赤松製成的。在這艘獨木舟的建造工作上，詹森扮演了一個重要的角色，而他的藝術作品帶給我們的，正是傳統與現代表現的融合，這將使夏威夷文化生意盎然並且持續成長。

A Hawaiian contemporary art

In 1975, Rocky Kaiouliokahihikoloehu Jensen formed a society of young Hawaiian artists who would stress "Hawaiianess" in the arts. To accomplish this, members were encouraged to study forms of traditional knowledge. Their contemporary art would be expressions of ancient learning. As Jensen expressed:

> *Culture is a living entity which should grow and change with time. Therefore to understand what we are today, we must first know and understand our past, for the solutions of today's problems lies therein. The form which culture takes today must have its roots in what has come before…. Only then can we give new meanings to the culture of the present and insure the security of our future.*

Jensen's art displayed here is made from the discavded spruce used to make the Hawai ìloa. Jensen had an important role in the construction of the canoe, and his art provides just the blend of tradition and modern expression that will keep the Hawaiian culture vibrant and growing.

洛基・詹森於比夏博物館建造夏威夷洛亞號

Rocky Ka'iouliokahihikolo'Ehu Jensen, construction of
Hawaiiloa at Bishop Museum

Native Hawaiian Culture and Arts Program 提供

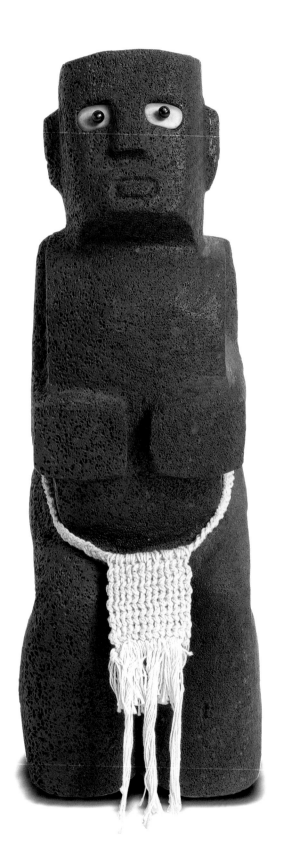

卡那羅亞

Kanaloa

L19 × W15 × H46cm

多孔玄武岩、長牙、纖維材料

Vesicular basalt, ivory, fiber

洛基・詹森 製作

Made by Rocky Ka'iouliokahihikolo'Ehu Jensen

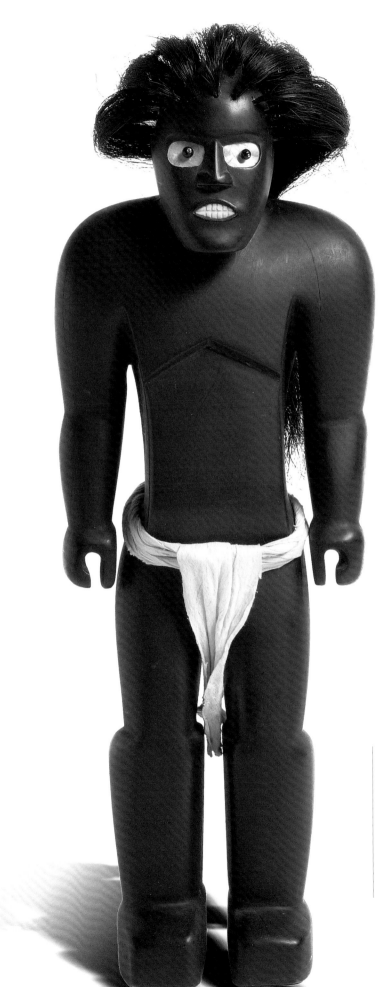

茂宜－阿－卡拉那
Maui-a-Kalana
L62 × W21 × H10cm

「歐希阿」、鑲嵌長牙與珠母貝、頭髮、纖維材料
Ōhi'a, ivory & mother-of-pearl inlay, hair, fiber

洛基‧詹森製作
Made by Rocky Ka'iouliokahihikolo'Ehu Jensen

馬哈納烏盧耶戶
Māhanauluehu
L57 × W20 × H44.5cm

卡馬尼、鑲嵌長牙與珠母貝、頭髮、纖維物質
Kamani, ivory & mother-of-pearl inlay, hair, fiber

洛基・詹森 製作
Made by Rocky Ka'iouliokahihikolo'Ehu Jensen

此三件雕像中的兩件，代表了玻里尼西亞或毛利的兩千年歷史。以玄武岩雕刻的這座卡那羅亞雕像是一個祖先神祇，祂的功績是帶領毛利人旅行，最後建立一個新國家。祂在玻里尼西亞人的宇宙演化論中是一位重要人物，也在一篇頌詩中被提到，此頌詩描述了在茂宜神紀元的兩千年前所發現的一片土地。由於祂與航行、發現之間具有強力關連，因此被視為海洋之神。

茂宜－阿－卡拉那是一位喜愛冒險的領航員，他在第一個千禧年之初，即開啟了一段從馬努阿、塔悟和薩摩亞開始的旅程，他遵循極為複雜的導航概念，他受稱頌的是：開始整個玻里尼西亞三角形區域內所有島嶼之移民定居，在他抵達之前，這些島嶼是無人居住的。

在太平洋區各地的故事與頌詩中，茂宜－阿－卡拉那的妻子馬哈納烏盧耶戶有許多不同的名字，全部名字都象徵她的後裔對她感受到的愛。她是最偉大的領航員茂宜－阿－卡拉那背後鼓舞的來源，從薩摩亞到太平洋內部的「摩納卡希寇」（指古老之洋）的旅程中，她協助他尋得航行之法。

這三尊雕像連同木製的雙舟獨木舟「夏威夷洛亞號」的建造，都是受夏威夷原民文化與藝術計畫所委託。

Two of the three images represent a Polynesian, or Maoli, history that is 2000 years old. Kanaloa, rendered in basalt is the ancestral deity credited with bringing the Maoli along a journey that resulted in the founding of a new nation. He is a predominant figure in all Polynesian cosmogony, being spoken of in chant as having discovered land two thousand years before the era of the god Maui. Because of his strong connection with navigation and discovery, he is considered god of the ocean,

Maui-a-Kalana is the adventurous navigator who initiated the journeys from Manuʻa, Taʻū, Sāmoa at the beginning of the first millennium. Following very sophisticated navigational concepts, he is credited with starting the settlement of all islands within the Polynesian triangle, which before his arrival were totally uninhabited.

In story and chants throughout the Pacific, Māhanauluehu, the wife of Maui-a-Kalana goes by many names, all symbolic of the love her descendants felt for her. She was the inspiration behind the great navigator, Maui-a-Kalana. She assisted him in discovering the method of travel from Sāmoa to the interior of the Pacific Ocean, Moana Kahiko.

The three images were commissioned by the Native Hawaiian Culture & Arts Program in conjunction with the building of the double-hulled wooden canoe, *Hawaiʻiloa*.

庫木黑類

Kumuhele

L124.5 × W44.5 × H58cm

寇阿木（相思樹）、西加赤杉木、纖維材料、珠母貝
Koa（*Acacia koa*）, Sitka spruce, metal, fiber, mother-of-pearl

洛基・詹森製作
Made by Rocky Ka'iouliokahihikolo'Ehu Jensen

庫木黑類涉及網綁技術，運用此技術將「連結橫木」結合在夏威夷式舷外浮桿獨木舟的船舷上，而選擇特定的網綁設計方式是「阿里夷奴夷」（高階酉長）的特權。「庫木」意謂著基礎或源頭，也指「編製之起始點」，「黑類」則是去綁或使其結合。

詹森知名的在於他這些技能：對實用事物的構成，鑒定其藝術複雜性，然後藉由將它們當作藝術來呈現，進而創造出表現法及溝通方法。庫木黑類所用的寇阿木和赤松木是1994年建造75英尺長（約2.3公尺）的夏威夷洛亞號時的剩料；順從了夏威夷的傳統，激起了天然材料的明智運用，於是，棄置的木塊便轉換成美麗的東西。

Kumuhele refers to the lashing that attached the "canoe spreader" to the gunnels on a Hawaiian outrigger canoe. The choice of a particular lashing design was the privilege of the *ali'i nui* (high chiefs). *Kumu* means foundation or source, and also refers to the "starting point of plaiting." *Hele* means to tie or to bind.

Jensen is known for his skill in taking components of utilitarian things, identifying their artistic intricacies, then creating expression and communication by rendering them as art. The koa and spruce in Kumuhele are remnants of the 75 foot double - hull, ***Hawai'iloa*** built in 1994. Pieces that were discarded were turned into beauty following a Hawaiian tradition that prompted judicious use of natural materials.

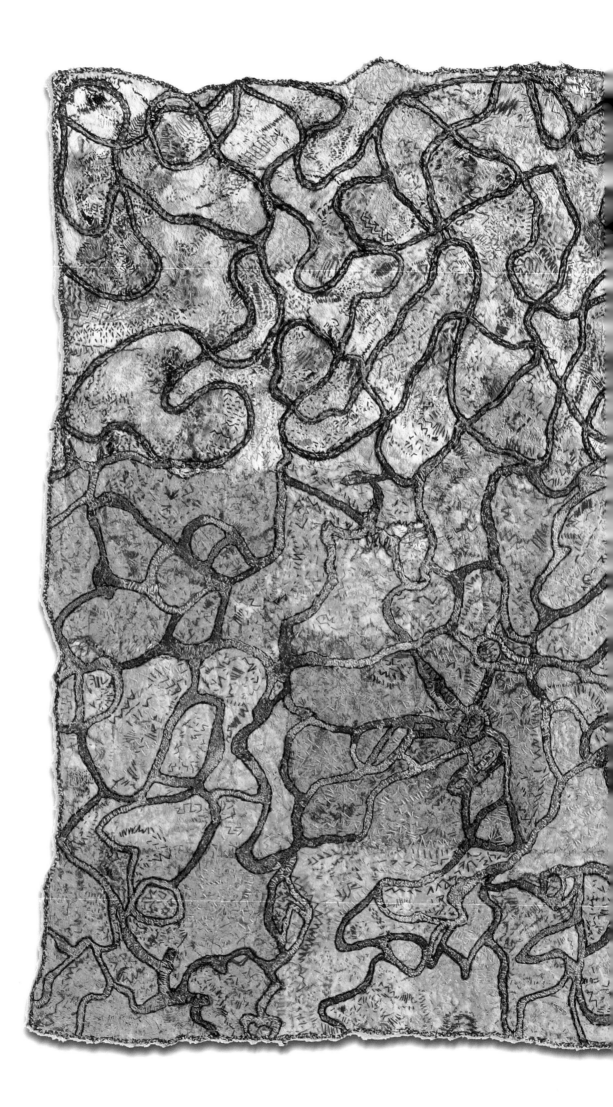

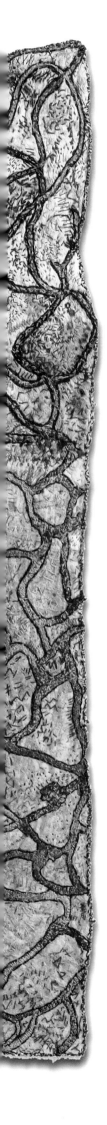

現代樹皮布藝術

Mele Hoʻala, modern barkcloth art

L120 × W89cm

布料、植物纖維（構樹）
Fabric, plant fiber(paper mulberry)

瑪緹娜‧羅賓‧聶弗
Made by Martina Robin Neveu

現代藝術家已精鍊於「卡帕」（樹皮布）製作的技術，並且
創造著含括此傳統材料的令人興奮之藝術品。這件近期作品
是一位來自西班牙的訪客在夏威夷製作的，聶弗是位知名藝
術家，她在忙碌的生活中騰出時間來研究並教導卡帕製作的
藝術。她在夏威夷渡過了夏天的幾個月，運用此夏威夷樹皮
布來學習、創作。
美樂侯阿拉與一首用來喚醒酋長的歌有關。
夏威夷的傳統技藝再現，並在世界其他地方受到讚揚。

Modern artists have mastered the techniques of kapa (barkcloth)
making, and are now creating exciting art that incorporating this
traditional material. This recent piece was made in Hawaiʻi by a
visitor from Spain. Robin Neveu is a well-known artist who
makes time in her busy life to study and teach the art of making
kapa. She spends summer months in Hawaiʻi learning and creating
with this Hawaiian barkcloth.

Mele hoʻala refers to a song used to wake a chief.

Hawaiian traditional skills have been rediscovered, and are
celebrated in other parts of the world.

反思與同理
Reflection and Empathy

比夏博物館的珍藏述說著，從原始南島部落到今天，夏威夷成為太平洋中民族熔爐和樂園的精彩傳奇故事。

臺灣與夏威夷的原住民同為「南島語系」家族的一員，從歷史來看，我們曾有同源的關係，分享著一些共同的文化特質。本次特展除引領大家欣賞比夏博物館的珍貴典藏，也希望藉此與台灣類似的歷史和社會發展過程相比較。

自二十世紀末以來，文化多元已成為普世尊崇的價值，世人日益重視對思想、信仰、價值和生活方式差異的基本尊重與保護。在此一社會發展趨勢下，如何保存與重塑原住民傳統文化，已成為當代社會的重要議題之一。

無論是夏威夷或是台灣原住民的各種傳統重建，背後都隱含了深沉的價值和努力。期望國人在欣賞此次特展之餘，也能對臺灣原住民文化價值多些反思，進而增廣面對多元文化所應有的認識和胸襟。

Treasures from the Bishop Museum tell us a mysterous story about the changes of the Hawaii Islands from a land of aboriginal tribes to a paradise of the ethnic melting pot of the Pacific.

The Hawaiian and Taiwanese indigenes speak the same Austronesian languages and share the same cultural characteristics. In addition to appreciate the precious collections from the Bishop Museum, this exhibit would like to lead the visitors to understand and to compare the similarity of the processes of the historical and social development between Hawaii and Taiwan.

Multiculturalism, an idea that people should respect and protect the diversity of thoughts, beliefs, values and life styles, has become a worldwide value by the end of the twentieth century. Nowadays, how to preserve and reconstruct the cultural traditions of the indigenous peoples has become one of the most important issues.

There are deep values hidden behind the various efforts attempting to reconstruct the indigenous cultures, no matter Hawaiians or Taiwanese. We hope that our visitors would be able to contemplate and to reflect on the real value of indigenous traditions in Taiwan through seeing this exhibition, and furthermore to broaden their vision and receptivity while facing the diversity of cultures.

凡例

一、本特刊所有文物均為「美國夏威夷比夏博物館」藏品，特選本館與該館
　　合作之「檀島傳奇」特展中之展出文物 133 組件介紹。

二、本書內容之編排分為二部分，第一部份為圖版與圖說，第二部分為藏品
　　圖版與插圖的相關索引。

三、本特刊依特展展出單元依序編排。圖說文字執筆者為比夏博物館 Betty
　　Kam副館長、臧振華先生 (p.019)、張至善先生 (p.211)。

四、藏品尺寸說明之排列順序為長度╳寬度╳高度，例如：120x78x12。直
　　徑以英文縮寫 Dia 表示。

五、本特刊內所引用之插圖、照片來源與內容、年代，可利用「插圖索引」
　　進行查詢。

誌謝

本特展緣起於92年12月9日，前館長臧振華先生、研究典藏組林志興主任與公共服務組研究助理徐雨村先生前往夏威夷考察南島文化園區設置工作，期間拜訪夏威夷比夏博物館，並會晤總裁布朗博士（Dr. Bill Brown），就雙方合作 事宜進行會談。93年2月1日史前館與比夏博物館簽訂五年共同合作備忘錄，成為姊妹館，計畫於未來共同推動藏品、特展與館員之交流，並推動學術研究、展演活動、教育推廣與行銷等事務。93年9月11日至23日，前副館長崔瑞明先生、展示教育組喬宗忞主任與研究典藏組研究助理葉前錦小姐前往夏威夷，洽談合作籌劃特展與特展內容架構相關事宜。94年獲教育部補助，進行「檀島傳奇－從羽神到熔爐」特展設計與施作，94年8月份，因業務調整，本項特展業務由喬宗忞主任轉交由展示教育組張至善先生後續執行。本特展自94年12月11日開展，至95年9月1日順利閉幕。由於下列參與人員之協助，本次特展得以順利完成，在此表達誠摯之謝意。

特別感謝

策劃	臧振華・崔瑞明・林志興・喬宗忞・徐雨村
展示架構形成	Betty Kam（比夏博物館）・喬宗忞
展示內容	Betty Kam・張至善
策展及協調	張至善
策展助理	林妙香
文稿審訂	郭佩宜
英文翻譯	林妙香
展示設計製作	津魚有限公司
標本狀況報告	比夏博物館・葉前錦・夏麗芳
標本點交	徐雨村・葉前錦・夏麗芳・張至善・劉世龍
標本開箱與復運包裝	林怡君・鄭文伶・陳金震・夏麗芳・葉前錦
標本上架	方鈞瑋・林怡君・林娜鈴・林健華・洪健二・陳曉燕・許益暢・袁素梅・夏麗芳・葉前錦・鄭文伶・蔡志鵬（依筆畫順序）
標本運輸	海灣國際股份有限公司・林建成・劉世龍
標本攝影	涂寬裕
攝影助理	林怡如・林怡君・鄭文伶・陳金震
工作影像紀錄	夏麗芳・葉前錦
開幕典禮	邱瓊儀・傅鳳琴・李佳穎・廖碧蘭・黃玫瑋-
教育活動	張至善・袁素梅・楊素琪
解說活動	公共服務組
發包作業	楊宗瑋・魯玉玲・黃玉燕

太平洋各地的錛與斧

Adzes from throughout the Pacific

圖版索引 PLATE INDEX

P.022

石斧

Stone axe

New Britain, Papua New Guinea

L64.5 × W17 cm

From the Field Museum of Chicago in 1926

P.023

有柄石斧

Hafted stone adze

Papua New Guinea

L64 × W28 cm

From W. Steffan in 1965

P.023

有柄石斧

Hafted stone adze

Papua New Guinea

L70 × W64 cm

Received in 1989

P.024

有柄硨磲蛤殼斧

Tridacna shell adze, hafted,

Gilbert Islands, Kiribati

L40 × W22 cm

Purchased in 1900

P.024

有柄硨磲蛤殼斧

Tridacna shell adze, hafted,

Truk, Federated States of Micronesia

L55 × W33 cm

From H. Hornbostel in 1924

P.025

有柄硨磲蛤殼斧

Tridacna shell adze, hafted,

Sikaiana, Solomon Islands (Polynesian Outlier)

L69.5 × W34 cm

From T. Crocker in 1933

P.025

有柄石錛

Hafted adze

Society Islands

L50 × W20.5 cm

Purchased in 1927

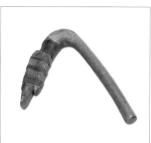

P.026

有柄石斧

Hafted adze with coconut sheath,

Marquesas

L48 × W35.5 cm

Purchased in 1940

P.026

有柄石錛

Hafted adze

Rarotonga, Cook Islands

L47 × W17.5 cm

From T. Dranga in 1966

P.027

有柄石錛

Hafted adze

Tahiti, Society Islands

L41 × W30.5 cm

ABCFM Collection, received in 1895

P.027

有柄石錛

Hafted adze

Hawaiian Islands

L53 × W21 cm

Bishop Museum Collection, received in 1986

玻里尼西亞的魚鉤和誘餌
Polynesian fish hooks and lures

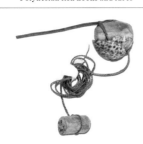

P.029
章魚誘餌
Octopus lure
24.5 × 6cm
typical of Samoa
found in the Society Islands

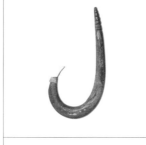

P.032
魚鉤
Fishhook
Samoa
26.5 × 15.5cm
Kapi`olani-Kalaniana`ole Collection,
received in 1923

P.029
章魚誘餌
Octopus lure,
Society Islands
20.5 × 6cm
From Mrs. M.D. Hendricks in 1902

P.033
魚鉤
Fishhook
Hawai`i
5 × 3.3cm
Ruth Ke`elikōlani Collection, received in 1885

P.029
章魚誘餌
Octopus lure
37.5 × 7.5cm
Society Islands
From the Santa Barbara Museum of
Natural History in 1979

P.033
魚鉤
Fishhook
Hawai`i
5 × 3.2cm
From A.L.C. Atkinson in 1925

P.030
魚誘餌
Fish lure
Tonga
8 × 1.5cm
From I.P. Jagger in 1964

P.033
魚鉤
Fishhook
Hawai`i
5 × 2.5cm
From the Canterbury Museum in 1951

P.030
魚誘餌
Fish lure
Hawai`i
11.8 × 1.8cm
J.S. Emerson Collection, received in 1889

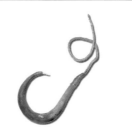

P.034
魚鉤
Fishhook
New Zealand
27 × 18.2cm
Eric Craig Collection, received in 1889

P.031
魚誘餌
Fish lure
Manahiki, Cook Islands
9.5 × 1.5cm
From Dr. and Mrs. P.H. Buck in 1930

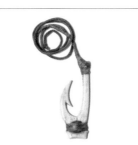

P.035
魚鉤
Fishhook
Hawai`i
9 × 3.6cm
From the Canterbury Museum in 1951

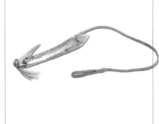

P.031
魚誘餌
Fish lure
Tuamotus
11.8 × 1.6cm
From K.P. Emory in 1930

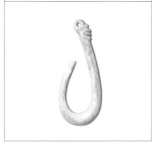

P.035
魚鉤
Fishhook
New Zealand
11.5 × 5cm
received in 1916

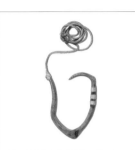

P.036

魚鉤

Fishhook

Cook Islands

25 × 19cm

From E. Beaglehole in 1935

P.037

魚鉤

Fishhook

New Zealand

5.4 × 2.9cm

From the Otago University
Museum in 1931

P.037

魚鉤

Fishhook

Rapanui

14 × 10.5cm

Purchased in 1920

P.044

布魯珊 神像

Hawaiian wooden image, Bloxam Image

H133 × 27 × 34cm

Replica of original at Bishop Museum

Made by Karl Axel de Flon and Fritz
Abplanalp

P.046

外阿奴耶奴耶 神像

Hawaiian wooden image, Waiänuenue

H160 × 49 × 29cm

Replica of original at Bishop Museum

Made by Karl Axel de Flon and Fritz
Abplanalp

P.048

庫卡伊里摩庫 神像

Hawaiian wooden image, *Kūkā`ilimoku*

H220 × 65 × 46cm

Replica of original at Bishop Museum

木缽和木盤
Wood bowls and platters

P.054

芋泥缽

`Umeke poi kou, poi bowl

H18 × Dia20 cm

P.059

洗手碗

Ipu holoi lima, finger bowls

L37 × W23 × H7cm

From A.F. Judd, received in 1921

P.054

木缽

`Umeke lä`au, wooden bowl

H11 × Dia23 cm

P.060

儲物缽

*Ipu lè`*l, storage bowl

H17 × Dia11.5cm

Hawaiian National Government
Museum Collection, received in 1891

P.054

碗

`Umeke mäna`ai, single serving bowl

H9.5 × Dia14 cm

Henriques Collection, received in 1932

P.055

芋泥缽

`Umeke poi, poi bowl

H27 × Dia31 cm

Received in 1976

P.056

木缽

`Umeke la`au, wooden bowl

H22 × Dia17 cm

From Mrs. A.H.B. Judd, received in 1914

P.058

小型芋泥板

Papa ku`i `ai, small poi board

L88 × W42 cm

P.059

洗手碗

Ipu holoi lima, finger bowls

L34 × W19 × H8cm

Received in 1970

椰子器皿
Coconut / Niu

石器
Stone implements

P.061

高腳杯

coconut goblets

H13.5 × Dia14cm

P.068

玄武岩石錛

Ko`i, adze (basalt)

L32.3 × W7 × T6cm

From C.R. Bishop Trust received in 1908

P.062

阿瓦杯

Olo awa, `awa cups

From C. Morris in 1952

P.068

玄武岩石錛

Ko`i, adze (basalt)

L7 × W2 × T4cm

Purchased in 1889

P.063

阿瓦杯

Olo awa, `awa cups

L19 × W10.5 × H7cm

P.069

玄武岩石錛

Ko`i, adze (basalt)

L27 × W8 × T4cm

Island of O`ahu, received in 1919

P.064

菸葉容器

Hano baka, tobacco containers

L12.4 × W5cm

Henriques Collection, received in 1932

P.070

錘

Sinker

L6 × W5 × T4.5cm

Island of O`ahu, from C. Rowe,

received in 1958

P.064

菸葉容器

Hano baka, tobacco containers

L8.6 × W9cm

J.S. Emerson Collection, received in 1889

P.070

錘

Sinker

L7 × W5 × T5cm

North Kona, Island of Hawai`i, from

W. Meinecke, received in 1955

P.065

煙斗

Ipu baka, tobacco pipe

88 × 42cm

J.S. Emerson Collection, received in 1889

P.070

錘

Sinker

L10 × W6 × T3cm

Necker Island, collected on the Tanager

Expedition, received in 1923

P.071

章魚誘餌

Lūhe`e, octopus lure

L21 × W7.5 × T12cm

P.072

玄武岩石杵

Pōhaku ku`i `ai, pounder (basalt)

H19 × Dia14cm (at base)

Received in 1989

P.076

玄武岩鏡

Kilo pōhaku, basalt mirrors

Dia21.3cm

J.S. Emerson Collection, received in 1889

P.073

玄武岩石杵

Pōhaku ku`i `ai, pounder (basalt)

H14 × W13cm × T8cm

Island of Kaua`i, received from W.C.
Bennett in 1929

P.077

玄武岩鏡

Kilo pōhaku, basalt mirrors

Dia13.7cm

Kapi`olani-Kalaniana`ole Collection,

received in 1923

P.074

投石器的石頭

`Alā o ka ma`a, slingstones

L8 × W4.5cm

Island of Kauai, purchased in 1889

P.074

投石器的石頭

`Alā o ka ma`a, slingstones

L6.5 × W5cm

From the W.T. Brigham Estate, received in 1926

P.075

缽

Poho pōhaku, bowls

H5 × Dia9.5cm

C.R. Bishop Trust, received in 1908

P.075

缽

Poho pōhaku, bowls

H6 × Dia7.5cm

Purchased in 1911

葫蘆製容器
Gourd containers

樹皮布打棒
I`e kuku, bark cloth beaters

P.082

葫蘆水瓶

Hue wai, gourd water bottle

H36 × Dia23cm

Queen Emma Collection, received in 1890

P.092

樹皮布打棒

I`e kuku, bark cloth beaters

L39 × W3.5 × H3.5cm

ABCFM Collection, received in 1895

P.083

葫蘆水瓶

Hue wai, gourd water bottle

H34 × Dia30cm

C.R. Bishop Trust, received in 1908

P.092

樹皮布打棒

I`e kuku, bark cloth beaters

L40 × W4.5 × H4.5cm

Island of Hawai`i, purchased in 1901

P.084

飾紋葫蘆

`Umeke pāwehe, decorated gourd

H19 × Dia22cm (at widest)

P.092

樹皮布打棒

I`e kuku, bark cloth beaters

L46.5 × W5 × H5cm

Island of Kaua`i, purchased in 1911

P.085

葫蘆容器

`Umeke pōhue, gourd container

L74 × Dia15cm

Kapi`olani-Kalaniana`ole Collection,

received in 1923

P.093

樹皮布打棒

I`e kuku, bark cloth beaters

L36 × W5 × H5cm

P.087

附椰子提繩的葫蘆容器

`Umeke pōhue, gourd bowl with coconut

carrier

H26.4 × Dia17.5cm

Island of Hawai`i, J.S. Emerson

Collection, received in 1889

P.093

樹皮布打棒

I`e kuku, bark cloth beaters

L43 × W4 × H4cm

P.094

竹製印模

`Ohe kāpala, bamboo stamps

small than L42 × W1.5cm

P.099

樹皮布樣品

Kapa samples

L55 × W42cm

P.094

樹皮布的畫線器

Lapa, kapa liners

small than L45 × W5cm

P.101

樹皮布樣品

Kapa samples

L58.5 × W42cm

P.095

樹皮布溝槽板

Papa hole kua`ula, grooved *kapa* board

L82 × W21 × H1cm

J.S. Emerson Collection, received in 1889

P.103

樹皮布樣品

Kapa samples

L59 × W34cm

P.095

溝槽器

Grooving implement

L32 × W7cm

Seth Andrews Collection, received in 1959

P.105

樹皮布樣品

Kapa samples

L80 × W45cm

P.096

樹皮布的砧板

Kua kuku, kapa anvil

L164 × W13 × H8cm

Hite Collection, received in 1986

P.097

缽和染料

Bowl and dye

H2.5 × Dia13cm

P.097

林投刷

Pandanus brush

L6cm

紡織、編織
Weaving and plaiting

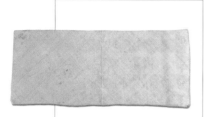

P.109

蓆子

Moena, mat

L142 × W67cm

Kapi'olani-Kalaniana'ole Collection,
received in 1923

P.110

扇子

Pe'ahi, fans

L: L37 × W24cm

R: L28.5 × W17.5cm

P.111

帽子

Päpale, hat

L30 × W36 × H10.5cm

P.113

瑪卡洛阿草蓆

Moena makaloa, makaloa mat

L56 × W44cm

From H. Cook in 1901

羽毛工藝

Feather work

P.117

羽毛披風

'Ahu'ula, feather cape

L82 × W59cm

ABCFM Collection, received in 1895

P.119

羽毛披風

'Ahu'ula, feather cape

L76 × W46cm

P.120

羽毛樣本

Feather samples

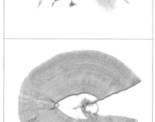

P.123

編網

Nae, netting

L59 × W52cm

Purchased in 1935

P.124

手持的「卡希利」

Kahili pa'a lima, hand kahili

H66cm

Received in 1958

P.125

「歐羅納」刮具

Olonä scrapers

Received in 1923

L23 × W9cm

P.125

「歐羅納」刮具

Olonä scrapers

Received in 1980

L15 × W6cm

P.125

「歐羅納」板

Olonä board

L206 × W9cm

P.126

長牙垂飾項鍊

Lei niho palaoa, necklace with
ivory pendant

L27 × W14 × H6cm

Queen Emma Collection, received
in 1895

P.131

葫蘆鼓

Ipu heke, gourd drums

H78 × Dia32cm

P.132

鼓

Pahu, drum

H29 × W17cm

Bishop Museum Collection (replica)

P.133

「庫佩耶」－踝飾

Kupe`e, ankle rattle

L40.5 × W27cm

Received from G. Gilman in 1894

P.134

音樂棒

Kāla`au, music sticks

上：L29 × W4cm

下：L40 × W3cm

P.135

葫蘆哨

Hōkiokio, gourd whistle

H7 × Cir17.5cm

消遣
Recreation

P.138

石製遊戲圓盤

`Ulu maika, stone game disks

H5 × Dia7.5cm

Maunaloa, Moloka`i, from C.M.
Cooke in 1924

P.147

獨木舟（模型）

Wa`a, canoe (model)

L60 × W30 × H12cm

Kapi`olani-Kalaniana`ole
Collection, received in 1923

P.138

石製遊戲圓盤

`Ulu maika, stone game disks

H2.5 × Dia5cm

Henriques Collection, received in 1932

P.149

獨木舟（模型）

Wa`a, canoe (model)

L30 × W20 × H72cm

Made by Francis Fujimoto, 1971

P.138

石製遊戲圓盤

`Ulu maika, stone game disks

H6.5 × Dia14cm

Kaupö, Maui, from Bottfeld and
Barth in 1937

P.150

長橇

Papa hölua, sled

L177 × W26 × H16cm

From D.L. Conkling in 1914

P.140

滑標

Moa pahe`e, sliding darts

L37 × Dia5cm

Hawaiian National Government Museum
Collection, received in 1901

L38.5 × Dia4cm

Received from G. Gilman, 1894

P.153

球與環的遊戲

Pala`ie, ball and loop game

L74cm   ball 5cm

Island of Kaua`i, from
Lili`uokalani in 1889

P.142

標

Pahe`e, dart

L72 × Dia2cm

From G. Davies in 1952

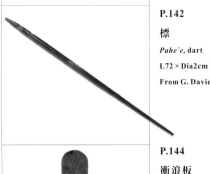

P.144

衝浪板

Papa he'e nalu, surfboard

L131 × W28 × T2cm

Woods Collection, received in 1935

早期夏威夷的生活
Life in early Hawai`i

P.161
羽環
Lei hulu manu, feather lei
L64 × W4cm
J.F. Woods Collection, received in 1924

P.163
刺青梳子
Tattooing comb
L28.6 × W6.2cm stiker L41.5 × W1.5cm
Made and loaned by Keone Nunes

P.165
庫佩耶，狗牙嘎嘎器
Küpe`e, dog teeth rattle
L36 × W27cm
Island of Kaua`i, purchased in 1911

P.167
葫蘆頭盔
Gourd helmet
H58 × Cir100cm
Modern replica

島嶼的轉變
Change in the Islands

P.171
臂膀用針鈕
Coat of arms brooch
Dia4.6cm
From Donna Kamellin in 1999

P.172
夏威夷錢幣的腰帶
Belt of Hawaiian coins
L77 × W3.7cm

P.175
「卡帕摩耶」
睡覺用的樹皮布
Kapa moe, sleeping kapa
L245 × W165cm
From H.T. Clarke in 1972

P.176
夏威夷襯墊絎縫枕頭
Hawaiian quilt pillow
L58.5 × W57cm
Made by Deborah "Kepola"
Umiamaka Kakalia
From Mrs. Herbert Y.C. Choy in
2005 (2005.045.001)

P.177
「夏威夷旗被」
Hawaiian flag quilt
L224.2 × W208.3cm
From Mrs. V.E. Schultz in 1960

P.179
棉被
Pïkake and Tuberose Quilt
L218.4 × W218.4cm
Made by Hannah Cummings Baker
From Lillian Macedo in 1984

夏威夷的當代藝術

A Hawaiian contemporary art

P.202

卡那羅亞

Kanaloa

L19 × W15 × H46cm

Vesicular basalt, ivory, fiber

Made by Rocky Ka'iouliokahihikolo 'Ehu Jensen

P.203

茂宜－阿－卡拉那

Maui-a-Kalana

L62 × W21 × H10cm

Ōhi'a, ivory & mother-of-pearl inlay, hair, fiber

Made by Rocky Ka'iouliokahihikolo'Ehu Jensen

P.204

馬哈納烏盧耶戶

Māhanauluehu

L57 × W20 × H44.5cm

Kamani, ivory & mother-of-pearl inlay, hair, fiber

Made by Rocky Ka'iouliokahihikolo 'Ehu Jensen

P.206

庫木黑類

Kumuhele

L124.5 × W44.5 × H58cm

Koa (*Acacia koa*) , Sitka spruce, metal, fiber, mother-of-pearl

Made by Rocky Ka'iouliokahihikolo 'Ehu Jensen

P.208

現代樹皮布藝術

Mele Ho`ala, modern barkcloth art

L120 × W89cm

Fabric, plant fiber (paper mulberry)

Made by Martina Robin Neveu

P.010

庫木里玻

The Kumulipo

Carl F. K. Pao

將夏威夷行銷到全世界

Selling Hawai`i to the world.

P.189

姆姆

Holokū style *mu`umu`u*

H231 × L672cm

From L.D. Klabau in 1999

P.189

姆姆

Holokū style *mu`umu`u*

H200 × L750cm

From Donald and Dorothea Woodrum in 1993

P.191

`Ukulele

L59 × W19cm

Made by Leonardo Nunes

From the Jeanne Race Woodbury Trust in 2003

P.194

吉他

Coconut *kīkā,* guitar

L83.5 × W29.7cm

From A.G. Cox and F.P Cox in 1977

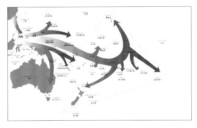

插圖索引 ILLUSTRATION INDEX

P.052

Ioane（右）和家人在吃芋泥

Ioane (rt.) and family eating poi, Hawaiï
ca. 1885

P.066

擣製芋泥的夏威夷男子們

Hawaiian men pounding poi beside *hale pili* (grass house), Hawaiï

P.078

搬運葫蘆的夏威夷人

Hawaiian man calabash carrier, Hawaiï
Color postcard.
Henry W. Henshaw,
ca. 1895

P.080

夏威夷男子擣製芋泥

Hawaiian man pounding poi, Hawaiï

P.106

編織林投蓆

Kihaa Piilani weaving lauhala mat, Molokai, Hawaiï

Ray Jerome Baker. Ray Jerome Baker Collection.

ca. 1912

P.114
伊伊蜜鳥
'I'iwi *Vestiaria coccinea*, Hawai'i.
Hand-colored lithograph.
Newman West. From: Scott B. Wilson and A. H. Evans, Aves Hawaiienses:
The Birds of the Sandwich Islands [Hawai'i](London:1890-1899), pg9, pl. I.
F.W. Frohawk.
December 1890

P.127

戴著lei niho palaoa的女子
Hawaiian woman wearing a *lei niho palaoa*
(ivory and braided human hair hook pendant), a sign of chiefly rank, Hawaiï
Image Number: CP 74465

P.129

呼拉舞者

Hula dancers posed in photo studio, Hawaiï

ca. 1890

P.130

比夏博物館夏威夷廳的樂舞表演

Pele Pukui Suganuma and Kaupena Wong performing in Hawaiian Hall,
Bishop Museum, Honolulu, Hawaiï
1958

P.136

在庫克船長面前舉行的拳擊競賽

Boxing match before Capt. Cook

John Webber

P.139

玩夏威夷保齡球

Playing *ulu maika*

1950

P.141

玩滑標

Playing *Moa pahe`e*

1950

P.143

拋網叉魚的夏威夷漁夫

Hawaiian throw net and spear fishermen, Kealakekua Bay, Hawaiï

Alonzo Gartley

ca. 1900-1910

P.145

夏威夷男子與衝浪板

Native Hawaiian man with surfboard, Waikiki, Honolulu, Hawaiï

Diamond Head in background.

Ca.1897-1901

P.150

侯路阿騎乘示範

Man demonstrating use of Hawaiian *holua* sled,

Pan Pacific Press Bureau

P.154

詹姆士・庫克船長

"Captain James Cook." Engraving.

Artist: Nathaniel Dance.

Engraver: T.K. Sherwin.

1779

P.156

1778年，夏威夷之歐尼豪島景觀

View of Oneehow, one of the Sandwich Islands, 1778

William Ellis

P.156

1778年，夏威夷之阿托瓦島景觀，阿托威與國王山

Views of Atowa, one of the Sandwich Isles, Atowi and the King's Mount, 1778

William Ellis

P.157

1779年，歐維豪西側之部份景觀，位於夏威夷之歐外黑島

Part of the west side of Owhehow, one of the Sandwich Islands, Owhyhee, 1779

William Ellis

P.158

1779年，在夏威夷對庫克的進貢

An offering before Captain Cook in the Sandwich Islands, 1779

Ink and watercolor wash by John Webber

P.160

夏威夷的女孩

A girl of the Sandwich Islands

John Webber

P.161

歐歐鳥

'O-O' *Acrulocercus nobilis*, Hawaiï

Hand-colored lithograph.

P.162

夏威夷半邊臉刺青的男人

Man of the Sandwich Islands, half face tattooed

John Webber

P.164

夏威夷跳舞的男子，1780年

Man of the Sandwich Islands, dancing, ca. 1780

John Webber

P.166

夏威夷的獨木舟，戴防護面具的槳手們

A canoe of the Sandwich Islands, the rowers masked

Engraving based on art by John Webber

P.168

卡美哈美哈大帝

Kamehameha the Great

P.176

Debbie Kepola Kakalia製被

Debbie Kepola Kakalia, Hawaiian quilting instructor quilting at Atherton Hal
Bishop Museum, Honolulu, Hawaiï

Ben Patnoi

1981

P.177

製作夏威夷被的女人們

Women making Hawaiian quilt at Ala Moana Park, Waikīkī, Honolulu, Hawaiï

Tai Sing Loo

1949

P.180

檀香山的日本家庭

Japanese man, women, and child with their pet dog, Honolulu, Hawaiï

Usaku Teragawachi. Usaku Teragawachi Collection.

ca. 1920

P.183

Chun Poon (第一排右側)一家人

Chun Poon family (lt.-rt.)

Laurence E. Edgeworth

ca. 1900

P.184

農場衣物

Plantation clothing

P.186

菜單封面

Menu covers

1930

P.188

兩位呼拉舞者

Hula dancers Lily Padeken Wai (right) and Leolani Blaisdell (left),

at the Royal Hawaiian Hotel, Waikīkī, Honolulu, Hawaiï

ca. 1950

P.190

宮廷呼拉舞者

Hawaiian hula dancers from King Kalakaua's court, Hawaiï; Pauahi in center.

Joaquin A. Gonsalves

ca. 1885

P.192

手拿四弦琴的夏威夷女子

Hawaiian woman with ukulele, Hawaiï

Cyanotype.

Alfred Mitchell

1886

P.193

穿戴花環的夏威夷女子

Hawaiian woman wearing lei, Hawaiï

n.d.

P.196

查理斯・理德・比夏和伯妮絲・帕娃希・比夏

Charles Reed and Bernice Pauahi Bishop.

Bradley & Rulofson,

P.196

夏威夷檀香山比夏博物館

Bishop Museum, Honolulu, Hawaiï

2005

P.198

夏威夷洛亞號細部

Detail of Hawaiïloa

Native Hawaiian Culture and Arts Program

P.198

接近完成階段的夏威夷洛亞號

Hawaiiloa in its completing phase of construction

Native Hawaiian Culture and Arts Program

P.199

展廳一偶

The Exhibition.

NMP, 國立臺灣史前文化博物館

P.200

洛基‧詹森

Rocky Ka'iouliokahihikolo'Ehu Jensen, construction of *Hawaiïloa* at Bishop Museum

Native Hawaiian Culture and Arts Program

P.201

製作夏威夷洛亞號的材料

The Woods.

Native Hawaiian Culture And Arts Program

P.210

布農族女子

The Bunun Woman

NMP, 國立臺灣史前文化博物館

從羽神到熔爐
The Mystreious Hawai'i
From the Feathered Gods the Melting Pot

展示廳實況　THE EXHIBITION GALLERY

從羽神到熔爐

檀島傳奇
The Mysterious Hawai'i
From the Feathered Gods to the Melting Pot

國家圖書館出版品預行編目資料

檀島傳奇－從羽神到熔爐特刊= The Mysterious Hawai'i－From the Feathered Gods to the Melting Pot /國立臺灣史前文化博物館出版品編輯委員會編輯；林妙香英文翻譯. -- 初版.-- 臺東市：史前文化博物館，民95　　　面；　公分.--

含索引 ISBN 978-986-00-7352-2 （精裝）. --

ISBN 978-986-00-7353-9 （平裝）. --

1.夏威夷　文化 2.南島民族

752.793　　　　　　　　　　　　　　　95022592

檀島傳奇－從羽神到熔爐
The Mysterious Hawai'i　From the Feathered Gods to the Melting Pot

展覽名稱 / 檀島傳奇－從羽神到熔爐

發行人 / 浦忠成

編輯 / 國立臺灣史前文化博物館出版品編輯委員會

執行編輯 / 張至善

文稿撰寫 /Betty Kam（比夏博物館）

英文翻譯 / 林妙香

開幕典禮執行 / 邱瓊儀‧傅鳳琴‧李佳穎‧廖碧蘭‧黃玫瑋

展示設計 / 津魚有限公司

攝影 / 涂寬裕

美術設計 / 謝忠雄（老二哲學簡單設計）

印刷 / 中原造像股份有限公司

發行所 / 國立臺灣史前文化博物館

地址 / 950臺東市豐田里博物館路1號

電話 / 886-89-381166

傳真 / 886-89-381199

出版日期 / 中華民國九十五年十二月（初版）

統一編號 / 1009503288

ISBN / 978-986-00-7352-2（精裝）

ISBN / 978-986-00-7353-9（平裝）

定價　新臺幣 1200 元（精裝）

新臺幣 1000 元（平裝）

從羽神到熔爐

檀島傳奇

The Mystreious Hawai'i
From the Feathered Gods the Melting Pot

國立臺灣史前文化博物館
NATIONAL MUSEUM OF PREHISTORY